RISK AND 'THE OTHER'

From earthquakes to epidemics, nuclear to industrial accidents, the mass media continually bring into our daily lives the awareness of risk. But how do people respond to this ever-increasing awareness? How do people cope with living in what has been termed the 'risk society'? This book attempts to explain how, within a given social and cultural context, individuals make sense of impending crisis. In particular, it explains the widespread sense of personal invulnerability when faced with risk: the 'not me' factor. Using a social psychological framework it highlights emotional factors which are a key component of responses to risk that have hitherto been neglected due to the tendency of much psychological work on risk to concentrate almost exclusively on cognitive information processing.

This book will appeal to an international audience of postgraduates, academics and researchers in the areas of risk, psychology, medical anthropology and psychoanalytic studies.

Hélène Joffe is a Lecturer in Psychology at University College London. She has published extensively on risk.

D0026984

Risk and 'the other'

Hélène Joffe

CAMBRIDGE
UNIVERSITY PRESS

PUBLISHED BY THE PRESS SYNDICATE OF THE UNIVERSITY OF CAMBRIDGE
The Pitt Building, Trumpington Street, Cambridge, United Kingdom

CAMBRIDGE UNIVERSITY PRESS
The Edinburgh Building, Cambridge CB2 2RU, UK
http://www.cup.cam.ac.uk
40 West 20th Street, New York NY 10011-4211, USA   http://www.cup.org
10 Stamford Road, Oakleigh, Melbourne 3166, Australia

First published 1999

Printed in the United Kingdom at the University Press, Cambridge

Tyeset in Plantin 10 on 12 point   [CE]

A catalogue record for this book is available from the British Library

Library of Congress cataloguing in publication data
Joffe, Hélène.
Risk and 'the other' / Hélène Joffe.
    p.   cm.
Includes bibliographical references and index.
ISBN 0 521 66009 2 (hardback). – ISBN 0 521 66969 3 (paperback)
1. Risk perception.   2. Social psychology.
3. Other minds (Theory of knowledge)   I. Title.
HM256.J63   1999
302'.12 – dc21   99–13648   CIP

ISBN 0 521 66009 2 hardback
ISBN 0 521 66969 3 paperback

Contents

Preface

The framework which I develop in this book has evolved from my cross-cultural study of responses to AIDS in the first decade of its advent (Joffe, 1996a, 1996b). The findings resonated with a massive amount of work on other risks, across many of the social sciences, which showed that people respond 'not me', 'not my group', 'others are to blame' when initially faced with potential crises. It is crucial to clarify, from the outset, that this response runs alongside other risk-related thoughts and strategies, be they practical actions to avoid being affected, or religious, magical or representational strategies. However, my impetus to write the book stems from a desire to develop an understanding of the 'not me – other' facet of the response to a vast range of imminent dangers. I devote considerable attention to establishing its widespread nature, and to forging a framework with which to explain it.

The book begins with an exposition of the contemporary Western milieu, in which risks form a key aspect of daily experience. A goal of the book is to emphasise the ways in which lay thinkers make sense of what sociologists term the 'risk society'. Existing data concerning human responses to a range of risks are explored. Insights from psychology, anthropology, history and cultural theory are utilised to demonstrate the extensive nature of the 'not me – others' response. These disciplines are drawn upon in order to build up a composite picture of how 'the other' is represented in an ongoing manner by individuals, groups, communities and societies. In particular, the dual dehumanised-desired representation of 'the other', which has subtly permeated thinking across historical periods and cultures, becomes intensified at times of imminent danger. I provide a detailed account of my study of cross-cultural responses to the risk of AIDS in order to demonstrate how individuals protect their identities by holding representations which link potential crises to 'the other' in terms of their own group identity positionings. This not only results in a widespread sense of invulnerability to the risk, but also contributes to a sense of spoiled identity in those group members who are linked with the threat in the dominant representations.

Evidence from the social sciences indicates that simultaneous to imagining that *others* engineer their own bitter destinies, the majority of people in a society are able to carve a space of invulnerability for themselves. Complementing broader, social scientific inquiries, empirical work on the 'not me' response from the cognitive 'optimistic bias' tradition yields robust findings concerning the 'not me' response to a vast array of health and safety risks. This evidence is advantageous in terms of the concern of the book, since it corroborates data which emerge from the other approaches. However, the explanations offered for 'optimistic bias' reveal the fault lines of purely cognitive theory. Having exposed the problems inherent in conceptualising the individual as a faulty information processor, I suggest pathways for moving beyond this purely cognitive orientation towards the psyche.

The framework which I develop for understanding the 'not me – others' response is infused with emotion, with symbolisation and with a focus on unconscious processes. Psycho-dynamic and social representational tenets are integrated into a distinctive social psychological approach which is able to explain the forces at work when people respond to imminent danger. The role of subjectivity, of symbols and of emotional motivations has been severely underplayed in the contemporary risk literature. I accentuate aspects of the burgeoning literature on the emotions relevant to the response to potential danger in the hope that future work will consolidate this link. The book draws to a close with an examination of the extent to which responses to risks transform over time, followed by exploration of the extent to which the framework forged can be applied across the range of risks.

Acknowledgements

I would like to thank Rob Farr for early, academic guidance and inspiration. I am grateful to Jane Gregory, Christian Staerklé, Lisa Fishbayn, Alain Giami and Peter Harris for reading draft chapters and for providing valuable commentaries. The anonymous reviewers of the text provided excellent suggestions, for which I am most appreciative. Thanks to Benoît Monin Morandat and Georgina Haarhoff for spending summers gathering material for me. For high levels of encouragement and efficiency at Cambridge University Press my thanks to Catherine Max, Elizabeth Howard, Sarah Caro and Christine Firth. Finally, for the emotional support which helped me to write this, my gratitude to Adam Jones and to Anne Harrison.

1   Responses to risks: an introduction

In this book I forge a framework for exploring people's responses to risks including epidemic illnesses, nuclear threats, industrial accidents, wars and hurricanes. The risks which form the focus of the book threaten to strike large numbers of people quite suddenly. However, I show that there is continuity between how these mass threats and the more commonplace risks, such as having a car accident or heart disease, are apprehended.

The human response to such dangers has been explored in disciplines ranging from anthropology to cultural theory, from history to psychology. One common finding arises: people respond 'not me', 'not my group', 'others are to blame' when initially faced with risks. This book examines the link made between risks and 'the other'. It demonstrates that people tend to attain a sense of personal invulnerability to risk by externalising the threat. It also explores the effect of this process on those 'others' who are linked to the potential danger.

The roots of the 'not me – others' phenomenon are viewed differently in each discipline. The social scientific study of people's responses to risk tends to focus on either their narrow cognitive or their broad socio-cultural roots. My approach slots into the gap between these two poles. It explains the subjective experience of risk, connecting this experience to broader social factors. It demonstrates how social forces become sedimented in inner experiences, how the 'we' becomes contained within the 'I'. The challenge is to draw on the rich body of data from the social scientific spectrum, to produce a robust social psychological framework for understanding the human response to potential mass crises.

A thriving post-disaster literature deals with how adversity is processed by individuals. This includes work on post-traumatic stress disorder and on the impact of social support on coping. I do not address these essentially clinical issues, nor the actions taken by people once disasters have struck. I focus on the processes at work when individuals who have not been directly affected by the danger think about the possibility of being affected, once it has been brought to their attention. Since it is often the mass media that act as the harbinger of these threats, a core element of my framework pertains to the circulation of knowledge about risks between the expert, media and lay realms.

I begin this chapter by drawing on contemporary anthropological and sociological approaches to the human response in the face of risks. This provides the springboard for the social psychological orientation of the book, which focuses on subjective responses to risks while recognising that the individual's response is embroiled in socio-cultural forces. The objective of the book is to advance understanding of how people cope with the plethora of dangers of which they are made aware by messages which emanate from the social environment. I contend that people control the anxiety evoked by danger by forming social representations which alleviate the worry by portraying 'others', rather than the self and the in-group, as the more deserving targets of danger.

The risk society

The impact of risks on society has provided much food for sociological and anthropological thought. In contemporary Western society, risks clamour for people's attention, according to anthropologists (Douglas, 1986, 1990) and sociologists (Beck, 1986/1992; Giddens, 1991). Even though the advancement of technology has supposedly provided a sense of mastery over the natural world, it has spawned an unprecedented *sense* of risk. By having ever increasing levels of expert knowledge about risks relayed to them by the mass media, lay people are constantly surrounded by images and words which bring danger to their awareness.

The mass media play a crucial role in heightening awareness of risks. The media's livelihood depends upon their ability to attract audiences. They can rely on the compelling nature of danger to hold people's attention. In order to make imminent dangers newsworthy, levels of alarm are magnified. Risks are particularly useful for the mass media since they are able to generate news in the absence of an event (Gregory and Miller, 1998). The danger that *might* occur provides the drama, as do the controversies and breakthroughs within the scientific community. The mass media have been dubbed the 'church of change'. Since they favour new events over the more stable elements of the human condition, mass risks provide appealing material for them (Minogue, 1998). Media portrayals raise the spectre of risks by relaying localised disasters, across the globe. Without the mass media many disasters would be known to just those involved, rather than penetrating the consciousness of billions of people the world over.

The perception of being surrounded by myriad threats also relates to the nature of numerous contemporary dangers. Many are not amenable to the senses (Mol and Spaargaren, 1993). Since people cannot rely on sensory information to detect them, risks may lurk anywhere. Only the experts can recognise them. One of the shocking elements of disasters such as Chernobyl, for example, is that the effects of radiation are not obvious. This is also true of the greenhouse effect and acid rain. In a milieu in which people cannot keep in touch with the plethora of recent developments, or have sensations that forewarn them of imminent dangers, experts are called upon to decipher the likelihood and magnitude of the danger. Yet expert judgement is shrouded in doubt. The mass media compel lay people to witness the uncertainty that characterises experts' assessments of risks. The general public has been confronted with uncertainty surrounding links between BSE and CJD (bovine spongiform encephalopathy and Creutzfeldt-Jakob disease). Former uncertainties include the link between HIV and AIDS (human immunodeficiency virus and acquired immune deficiency syndrome), as well as between nuclear fall-out and leukaemia. In addition to being encouraged to witness the disagreements among experts, lay people are made aware that there are human-made risks, such as that from nuclear power, which have spin-offs which surpass the knowhow of the experts who created them. This undermines the trust that can be placed with 'experts'. Their authority is by no means assured.

The combination of a high level of awareness of risk, and a lack of trust in the experts who might be relied upon for protection, creates an era of uncertainty and unease. The 'risk society' (Beck, 1986/1992) or 'risk climate' (Giddens, 1991) that result are extremely anxiety provoking for their members. One of the ways in which contemporary societies have tried to seize control over these circumstances is by making every attempt to calculate and to regulate dangers. Risks are represented as if they are systematically caused, statistically describable and, consequently, somewhat 'predictable' (Douglas, 1990). An attempt is made to 'colonize the future' (Giddens, 1991) by assessing the risks of the various situations that might arise, and putting insurance and surveillance systems into place to prevent future damage from them. The ultimate contemporary example of this is the predictive genetic testing which will become widely available in the West in the near future. This test will examine a sample of an individual's genetic material with the aim of producing information concerning the health-related future of the individual (Davison, 1996). People's genetic blueprint maps their predisposition to certain conditions. However, it does not necessarily determine whether these conditions will occur, and does not determine their timing or severity.

Therefore, the goal of testing is to allow individuals to plan a lifestyle in which they make all of the choices possible to diminish the chance of being affected by those conditions to which they are predisposed. The new genetic findings may have had very different repercussions. The discovery of the genetic bases of illness may have militated against the accentuation of the role of 'healthy choices' in ensuring health. Yet choice and control are stressed due to the profound effects of the ideology of individualism. From the 1970s onward, in both North America and Britain, individuals have been represented as entities who forge their own health-related destinies. Living a long life has been a do-it-yourself proposition (Crawford, 1984). Despite growth in knowledge concerning the predetermined nature of certain illnesses, modern Western societies continue to forge measures to maximise control over any changeable elements of this predisposition.

This is a very different orientation to danger from that which existed in pre-modern times. Although members of societies have always tried to take some form of control over the perils they faced (e.g. by magic), in pre-modern times fate and destiny were relied upon to shape people's futures. Events were experienced not in terms of causal, predictable relations but in terms of cosmic order. The very meaning of the contemporary word for danger – risk – refers to the probability of a (generally) negative outcome, accompanied by the magnitude of the damage which it will do. Danger, on the other hand, merely connotes peril.

By enveloping risks in the language of probability, one swathes the notion of danger in an aura of science (Douglas, 1992). Risk is merely danger dressed in modern clothes. Risk simply means 'danger from future damage',[1] yet the term 'risk' implies precision of calculation, which suggests objectivity and control. The term 'danger', I would argue, also evokes a far more emotive quality. It suggests that a menacing, threatening event is on the horizon. The concept of risk not only conceals the emotional facet of danger, but also obscures the value-laden nature of choices made in societies concerning risks. Risk-reduction policies claim to take their cue from the science of probability (e.g. see Backett et al., 1984).[2] Yet they reveal a more moralistic endeavour, one that routes dangers back to those responsible for them. Douglas points out that well-advertised risks tend to be those connected to moral principles and their legitimation. The greater accentuation of the danger posed by AIDS, rather than heart disease, since the early 1980s in the West, with the greater connection of AIDS to the morally laden domain, speaks to this point. The reported instances of the two types of illness do not justify this emphasis.

While seeking control over danger, via calculation and regulation, is an aspiration of the experts, Beck's (1996) very definition of the 'risk society' is one in which control is absent: 'The concept describes a phase of development of modern society in which the social, political, ecological and individual risks created by the momentum of innovation increasingly elude the control and protective institutions of industrial society' (Beck, 1996: 27). The notion of risk, by definition, presupposes that a decision can be made regarding how it is possible to avoid a hazard or danger. The incalculable threats of pre-industrial society are turned into calculable risks in industrial society, in line with the modern project of promoting rational control in all spheres of life. However, for Beck, the 'risk society' era follows the industrial phase of society and is different from this preceding form in that the risks – nuclear, chemical, ecological and those resulting from genetic engineering – are of a different order from industrial risks. They cannot be compensated for or insured against because they are not limited in time and space. This quality makes it difficult to hold entities accountable for them. The risks are also apprehended differently in that the public reflects upon them to a far greater degree than in previous times. This reflection produces an unprecedented public scepticism concerning the trust that can be placed in experts.

Despite these allusions to the perspective of the public and its mistrust of experts, Wynne (1996), a sociologist, argues that the risk society thesis has focused, almost exclusively, on expert knowledge. It contains a top-down dynamic. Lay people witness and take their cue from experts. According to Wynne, the notion of a public that constantly responds to and reflects upon expert agendas must be challenged. He contends that sociological work on the risk society has contained a gap in terms of specifying the dynamics of the lay dimension. Even Giddens' (1991) work, which deals with the intimate and interpersonal dimensions of lay knowledge, fails to elucidate the culturally rooted, collective facet. Contrary to these trends, Wynne highlights the way in which lay people forged the agenda of early nuclear issues in Britain. Lay people noticed excessive rates of childhood leukaemia in the vicinity of the Sellafield (formerly Windscale) nuclear reprocessing plant in the 1970s. Experts denied this until such time as the mass media took up the ideas of the lay people. This mass exposure of the problem prompted an official inquiry by the experts; this confirmed the excess of leukaemia which could not be attributed to other causes. The emphasis upon lay people setting the agenda is particularly valuable since it illustrates that lay people generate issues and act on society rather than constantly responding to expert agendas. Nevertheless, to refer to the process of the circulation of ideas in a society as being either top-down or bottom-up reflects an oversimplification. Even Wynne's characterisation of lay people identifying excessive leukaemia cases at Sellafield implicitly includes medical expertise, since it is medics who must have taken part in the identification of the individual cases of leukaemia. In order to capture the complexity of these dynamics, there is a need for a theory of the fluid interaction between lay and expert responses to risks. Some of the other issues raised by Wynne highlight further important aspects that an appropriate theory of the lay response to risk must encapsulate.

Wynne (1995) emphasises the need to reconstrue the 'public' as a plural entity: there are many 'publics' who apprehend the risks and they do so in line with issues of identity. In order to demonstrate how identity enters into the apprehension of risks, Wynne refers to the case of radiation workers at Sellafield who chose to maintain high levels of ignorance in relation to radiation risks because they did not want to threaten existing social arrangements in which certain experts were assigned the role of understanding the science of radiation and of thereby protecting the workers. A division of labour, as well as trust and dependency, were key features of the workers' responses to radiation risks. Wynne uses this case to support the notion that identity processes lie at the heart of people's responses to potential risks. While his work is useful in that it demonstrates that the broad brushstroke 'risk society' approach needs to consider the dynamic interaction of those with different roles in institutions, his approach is not infused by a theoretically driven understanding of the processes at work in identity construction. A focus on role allocation and the emotional dynamics of trust and dependency does not fully encompass or explain how people construct their orientation towards risks. In addition, the focus on the workers as a group irons out variability in their responses which may relate to their individual biographies, and to their group identities outside of the workplace. Insight into such factors provides knowledge of the workings of identity formation, as the theoretical position which I advocate will indicate.

Finally, another valuable debate which Wynne (1982) sets up is that between the advancement of rational rather than more symbolic and emotive responses to risks. He claims that within policy-making and within sociological work, emotional and symbolic facets are neglected. In relation to nuclear power, for example, its proponents have demanded that public debates evaluate the 'hard facts' alone, without reference to other realms. Yet for lay people, nuclear power is a highly emotive issue, one upon which the whole future of civilisation may rest. It carries a vast array of symbols, including that of scientific and technological hubris and of environmental destruction. Nuclear fall-out has also been associated with the destruction of people's health in the areas that surround nuclear plants. Again, while Wynne's work suggests exemplary avenues for exploration, coherent theory which allows for the development of these valuable angles, has not yet been developed within sociology.

A framework for understanding the individual's response to risks

Utilising the social psychological theory of social representations, in conjunction with certain psycho-dynamic ideas, the hiatus left by the various sociological positions concerning the nature of lay knowledge can be addressed. In the framework which I forge, the concern is with the culturally rooted, collective nature of the public knowledge of risks, as well as with the emotive and symbolic dimensions. My primary contention is that the personal shock evoked by mass risks sends people along a defensive pathway of representation. The 'risk society' does not necessarily leave people with a heightened state of anxiety, as Beck's and Giddens' work may suggest. Nor do humans rely exclusively upon surveillance and insurance systems to control this anxiety, to 'colonize the future'. Humans possess defensive mechanisms which protect them from unwelcome emotion. These defences are reflected in their representations of risks, which serve to control the anxiety evoked by the danger. The social psychological framework which I forge has the potential to strengthen the existing sociological ideas, allowing for reconciliation of the split between the more socially based dynamics and the more intimate, interpersonal levels of the response to risk.

Work on the subjective experience of risk in the context of the 'risk society' is surprisingly limited. Risk-related perceptions have been studied extensively in cognitive psychology without reference to the social environment. The psychological theory of 'optimistic bias' points to conclusive findings concerning how people interpret knowledge about risks. Most people imagine that they are less likely than their peers to be affected by a large array of risks. This area of research centres upon how people evaluate their own risk in comparison to how at risk they imagine others to be. People are found to be unrealistically optimistic in relation to their own susceptibility to dangers. Another area of cognitive psychology, that of judgement- and decision-making, evaluates the odds which people offer, in relation to their chances of becoming affected by a particular risk. The probabilities offered by lay people are often compared to scientific estimates, and the source of the errors made by lay people are explored. Both of these models focus on information processing problems which lead to the 'faults' observed. By positing purely cognitive origins to individuals' reactions to danger, they negate the role played by societal forces and are seldom drawn upon in social scientific debates about risk. While it is unsatisfactory to restrict a theory of the responses to risks to the cognitive realm, findings from this realm corroborate the 'not me – others' process which many social scientists identify in relation to imminent danger. This need not result from people being error-prone information processors. I explore the meanings which people make of risks. This inquiry provides evidence that both socio-cultural and emotional factors enter into the process of evaluating and experiencing risks. Rather than focusing on the disparity between lay and expert risk assessment, I examine the ways in which people prioritise protection of the self and in-group from threat over rational, objective assessments of danger.

The 'individual': on subjectivity

My concern is with what happens in the internal world of the individual who is faced with the threat of being affected by a disaster. An accusation of methodological individualism can be levelled at an approach which focuses on individual responses to mass risks. However, the point is that one can talk of individuals without individualising, without locating the origin of experience within the individual psyche. Processes that lie beyond the individual, and often beyond human awareness, play a key role in forging the individual's response to risks. A refrain throughout this book will be that social forces are embodied within the self: the 'we' is sedimented in the 'I'. The core theories on which the book draws – social representations theory and contemporary psychoanalysis – are integrated to explain this process.

My overall orientation is in keeping with the direction in which Henriques *et al.* (1984/1998) tried to propel psychology in the 1980s. They called for a focus on subjective experience, yet construed subjectivity as an entity shaped by social forces. It has not been taken up by many psychologists (see Billig, 1997 and Frosh, 1989a for notable exceptions), since the discursive model, which has catapulted to the forefront of social psychology, is not centrally concerned with subjective experience. Postmodern variants of discursive theory go as far as to eschew the notion of subjectivity completely. Michael (1994: 397) claims that 'there is no self'. According to this line of thought, those people who live in the West, under the influence of factors such as the electronic media, are postmodern beings. This type of being takes up many different subject positions. Rather than being a coherent entity, the 'self' is 'nomadic'. It moves between different perspectives and identities. Henriques *et al.* (1998) question this perspective succinctly and insightfully:

in this view the subject is composed of, or exists as, a set of multiple and contradictory positionings or subjectivities. But how are such fragments held together? Are we to assume . . . that the individual subject is simply the sum total of all positions in discourses since birth? If this is the case, what accounts for the continuity of the subject, and the subjective experience of identity? What accounts for the predictability of people's actions, as they repeatedly position themselves within particular discourses? Can people's wishes and desires be encompassed in an account of discursive relations? (Henriques *et al.*, 1998: 204).

These authors advocate a more unified subjectivity than that put forward in the postmodern stance. I adhere to the notion of a self that has a fairly stable sense of its position, and of internal, relatively consistent desires and wishes. The framework developed in this book is conceived as a late modern rather than as a postmodern enterprise. Both of the key theories upon which my approach draws are more modern than they are postmodern.

Why social representations theory?

The social representations framework, established by the social psychologist Serge Moscovici, provides a composite vision of the development of common-sense thinking. While sociologists such as Wynne suggest useful alleys regarding lay apprehension of risks, a unified theoretical position on lay thought emerges from the more psychologically rooted perspective. Social representations theory highlights and seeks to understand people's spontaneous philosophies about new societal events. The concern is with how different groups make meaning of events such as a newly identified epidemic or the threat of nuclear war. There is particular emphasis upon how lay theories come about and operate. The emphasis is wholly different from one which seeks to identify the faults made by lay thinkers in understanding risky situations, with the hope of rectifying mistaken thinking. This has been a dominant concern not only in cognitive psychology but also in the Public Understanding of Science (PUS) field. The PUS field's research agenda is centrally concerned with the measurement, explanation and finding of remedies for 'misunderstandings' of science and technology (Wynne, 1995). The approach assumes that the motivations for 'understanding' science are the same across experts and lay people. Primarily, the acquisition of 'objective knowledge', pertaining to the 'true facts', is imagined to be a common goal.

However, social representations theory proposes that the motivations which underpin 'risk perception' are not based upon a need for accurate information. Rather, people are motivated to represent the risks which they face in a way that protects them, and the groups with which they identify, from threat. They make meaning of the threat in line with self-protective motivations rather than with rational dictums. Social representations theory also emphasises communication, rather than internal information processing, when explaining how people set up their representations. It stresses the role of group affinities, rather than lone information processing, in shaping ideas. In the dialogue that goes on in pubs, on buses and around dinner tables, people shape their ideas about newly encountered threats in a way which fits with the ideas held by the groups with which they affiliate.[3]

Social representations theory is a social constructionist theory concerned with the specific forces at work in shaping understandings of new phenomena. It posits that the seeds of the representations of new phenomena which people create tend to lie in scientific interpretations, which get relayed from this reified, expert universe to the lay domain by the mass media. Therefore, the mass media play a critical role in feeding the dialogues between lay people, which establish their social representations. Initially experts, journalists and lay thinkers alike use old, familiar ideas in order to understand unfamiliar threats. They also draw upon the images and metaphors which circulate in the culture. By stamping new threats with the ideas associated with past dangers, the threat posed by the new, mysterious hazard is muffled. Assimilation in line with existing images and metaphors has a similar effect. The new event is absorbed in a way that reduces the fear which surrounds it, thereby protecting the sense of safety of the representor.

Unlike most discourse analysis, which is the more prevalent version of social constructionism in social psychology, social representations theory delves into the symbolisation inherent in a variety of representational genres. It does not elevate textual discourse over images and rituals, in order to explain how meaning is given to new events. The theory is also distinctive in comparison with discourse analysis in that it places great emphasis upon the specific group-based processes which are at work when individuals think about risks. Primarily, the group identifications of the individual shape which ideas are taken up from history and from the prevailing culture. When new risks are encountered, individuals draw on ideas and ways of thinking that originate within the groups with which they identify (Halbwachs, 1950; Moscovici, 1961/1976). Therefore risks evoke various group-linked responses within individuals.

This patterning also distinguishes social representations theory from postmodernist theorisation as a whole, which tends to accentuate the very diversity and fragmentation of human discourses. There is a degree of sharedness and coherence in the social representations held by members of naturally occurring social groups. The representations are unified by the common motivation to protect the in-group and self-identity via the representation. I have stated that unlike many social constructionist theories, social representations theory does not eschew the notion of subjectivity. Therefore psycho-dynamic theorisation can be drawn into the heart of the theory to allow for understanding of the interaction between the inner and outer worlds of the individual faced with a mass crisis.

Why psycho-dynamic theory?

Psycho-dynamic theory facilitates understanding of the roots of the social representations of risks which link danger with 'the other'. Anxiety, and the defence against it, are the key foci. My chosen psycho-dynamic outlook, drawn primarily from strands of object relations and Freudian theory, suggests pathways for synthesis of psychic and social processes. The object relations tradition is distinctive in that it posits that social forces lie at the root of the formation of mental life. People's mental lives are launched within *relationships* with primary caregivers. Representational life emerges from these early relationships. The unconscious representational structures which infants form there construct the bases of subsequent patterns of thought. Early representations tend to be orientated towards protection of the self from anxiety. In order to accomplish this, 'the other' becomes the repository of all that the infant seeks to push out from its own space for the purpose of protection. These early building blocks of what is to be associated with the self, versus with others, leave their mark on the developing individual. Political and social ideas acquired in the course of the lifespan augment the individual's notion of what can comfortably be associated with self and in-group, and what is unacceptable and must be flung out beyond their walls. Individuals learn which qualities and actions are acceptable from the norms of the societies in which they live. At times of potential threat, when levels of anxiety are particularly high, the early mechanism of defence reappears, and the 'other' becomes the target of a rich array of projections which contain those aspects of experience from which individuals seek to distance their selves.

This focus on mental life, on subjectivity, stands in contrast to broad brushstroke theories of risk-related thinking, such as some of the socio-logical and anthropological ideas mentioned above, which emphasise sweeping societal responses to risk, without taking heed of the indi-viduals who generate these responses. Even when lay thinking is taken into account, 'lay people' tend to be viewed as interest groups with various roles to carry out in the running of an institution or society. The psycho-dynamic focus on mental life also stands in stark contrast to the postmodern position in which there is certainly no coherent psychic space beneath the individual's veneer. Having denied the existence of the psychic core, it cannot be deemed a determining force in people's thoughts and actions.

Concern with individual subjectivity, with its roots in the uncon-scious, is rare within contemporary psychology, not least because of the dominance of the cognitive paradigm. Heider (1958), whose esteemed work is a cornerstone of the social cognition tradition, originally intro-duced the cognitive approach by stating: 'Our concern will be with "surface" matters, the events that occur in everyday life on a conscious level, rather than with unconscious processes studied by psychoanalysis in "depth" psychology. These intuitively understood and "obvious" human relations can, as we shall see, be just as challenging and psychologically significant as the deeper and stranger phenomena' (Heider 1958: 1). Interestingly, when he wrote this, Heider had to defend cognitive processes, emphasising their equal significance to unconscious processes. By the late 1990s, the scales had tipped in the opposite direction. The deeper, stranger phenomena are hardly given a mention in esteemed British and American psychology departments, other than to give students a flavour of a dim and distant past. In becoming interested in the surface, psychology has neglected the depths.

This has had serious consequences. The shift towards focusing on the conscious mind has distanced psychology from the study of emotional motivation and desire. Increasingly the emotions, once more, have become objects of study. Yet it is the biological, neurolo-gical, cognitive and discursive nature of the emotions that has been accentuated. The unconscious, subjective aspects of emotion, for the most part, have not been revisited. The framework which I develop revitalises this area. By taking heed of the new emotions literature, in both psychology and sociology, I endeavour to identify aspects which are relevant to the sense of invulnerability which arises at times of imminent crisis.

Quality checks

How can one check the quality of a framework, such as the one which I forge for studying human responses to risks? The power of any framework rests in the interpretation it allows (Silverman, 1993). Is it credible? Is it plausible? Is it robust? Does it incorporate the possibility of revision? Does it expand current thinking? Does it resonate with evidence found across a number of disciplines, and with data gleaned from various methodological standpoints? Ideally, if the framework contains considerable value and rigour, all of these questions should be answered in the affirmative. My exploration of evidence for the 'not me – others' phenomenon across a range of disciplines and methods, over subsequent chapters, is an attempt to convince the reader that the core phenomenon exists.[4] Of course those positioned in the different social sciences will be interested in different aspects of it, will want to check its validity by way of different methods and will have provisors in relation to the pervasiveness of the phenomenon. I want to reiterate that I am not making a claim for the 'not me – other' phenomenon being the sole response to imminent danger. It exists alongside other responses. Yet it is crucial, not least because the sense of invulnerability to the crisis which it promotes can stop people from taking appropriate actions in relation to the risks, and can set up self-blame and a spoiled sense of identity in members of groups designated as 'other' by the majority.

The useful 'depth'/'surface' division made by Heider (1958) points to the variable objects of study in psychology. Since science has variable objects, it also requires variable methods. Since I explore the meaning made of risks, with its unconscious and symbolic dimensions, the use of methods devised solely from observation of the conscious minds of individuals is inappropriate. I learn about the object of study – individuals' responses to risks – in a manner which befits this object. While taking into account data from a number of theoretical and empirical sources, I advocate depth interviewing of lay people, together with content analysis of the messages which exist in their social environments. This grants the researcher a sense of the meaning made of the risks. Analysis is theoretically driven, but is grounded in the pathways which lay thinkers follow in their interviews. The aim is to forge a framework that encompasses and explains the various facets of the 'not me – others' phenomenon that exists in relation to many risks.

Orientation of the book: resting between two poles

My framework fits into the space between the cognitive and socio-cultural poles of the spectrum of risk research. In the cognitive approach, which dominates the psychology of risk, lay people are presumed to face potential dangers rationally, yet to make cognitive errors due to the limitations of their information processing skills. Allusions to emotional states are oblique. The menace is removed from danger. It may be argued that prominent sociological works have approached risk with a similar orientation. Wynne (1996) criticises fellow sociologists Giddens and Beck for their rational, cognitivist reading of risk. Sociologists, with notable exceptions, have tended to focus on the 'risk society' as a monolithic environment, one in which all citizens are subject to raised levels of anxiety. This stance fails to explore how lay people imbibe knowledge of risks.

My concern is with the experience of the individual member of society, who must face a risk. Work which attempts to take both the socio-historical and individual experience of risk into account simultaneously is uncommon, though the insightful work of Gilman (1985a, 1988), a cultural historian, most closely approximates this position. He develops a theory of a widespread process that occurs in the West when people's levels of fear are raised, by imminent threats. Much of his work is located within the mental and physical health sphere. Gilman's focus is upon how Western images of disease are connected with a fear of collapse.[5] Yet people do not hold onto this fear. Rather, they externalise it. Once located outside of the self the fear is removed and it is the 'other', rather than the self, who faces catastrophe. Within his theory, the issue of control is central. Faced with having to interpret events such as epidemics, Westerners project a fear of loss of control onto 'others' who then become imbued with a tendency towards excess, such as excessive lasciviousness, which is felt to be absent within the self. The 'other' chosen as the target of projection is one who has already shown vulnerability to having collapsed. Gilman's model can be extended beyond the health sphere. It explains how responsibility for threats becomes displaced onto 'the other' who is then pathologised. By projecting the unwelcome links to the threat, the self is left pure, free from associations with the threat.

While Gilman's ideas have been a source of inspiration for me, they are different from my own in certain key respects. Firstly, my analysis points to the symmetry inherent in Western and non-Western responses to threat. Gilman's writing tends to focus on the projection of unwanted parts of the self in Western thinking.[6] I argue that even though the content of the representations is different, there is evidence of a 'not me – other' mechanism underlying responses in both contexts.

Secondly, Gilman's use of object relations theory is more circumscribed than my own since he draws on just one aspect: the splitting defence mechanism which originates in the first stage of the infant's life, with the attendant projective process. The aspect which he chooses, and then links in to the notion of stereotype, leads him to a more fixed theory of the response to crises. Further aspects of object relations theory indicate why representations of risk need not be of the 'not me – other' variety since later developments in the infant's representational system allow for a more complex, non-'stereotyped' apprehension of events. I explore the mechanism which facilitates this in the final chapter of the book.

Thirdly, Gilman's key focus is upon how the dynamics of the response to threat play out in images, be they artistic, those from medical textbooks or in public health campaigns. Gilman does not enter the world-views of lay thinkers directly. Arguably, these are more dynamic and changeable than the cultural artefacts upon which he bases his theory. However, both his approach, and the social representations approach to which I adhere, stress that the past stamps its mark on new representations of risks, but that representations also change over time. At times of crisis historical images are brought forward into the present, but they also get reshaped by contemporary currents.[7]

The work of Crawford (1994) is also complementary to my own in that it reconciles the individual and socio-cultural facets of responses to risk. Crawford's key concern is with the health sphere and with the ideologies that constitute health in the United States. He draws heavily upon the work of Gilman, and points to the relevance, for representations of health, of the bifurcation set up between the healthy, controlled self, and 'the other', who is the repository for connotations of out-of-control facets and can therefore be blamed for its own demise. He shows, convincingly, how this split is part of the identity work of North Americans. It leaves them with feelings of being protected. Unlike my own approach, he does not study the dynamic interaction between different group-based representations, such as that between groups accused of out-of-control behaviour and the dominant groups. I aim to demonstrate that such interactions are crucial for 'identity work'. Neither Crawford nor Gilman unpick the dynamic process of representation in a culture: the way in which people from differing groups take up risks brought to their attention via various forms of communication. The imagery explored by Gilman (1985a, 1985b) is a crucial aspect of representation, but we cannot know how humans read the images unless we invite them to tell us. Social representations theory makes a distinctive contribution to the theory of the circulation of new threats in a society by encompassing lay, media and scientific representations, and highlighting the 'identity work' accomplished by the process of representation.

Concluding remarks

The 'risk society' hypothesis proposes that contemporary, Western societies raise people's levels of anxieties by presenting them with litanies of risks over which experts have little control. The best known sociological writings on risk emphasise the *insurance and surveillance systems* that are put into place as a mechanism of exercising control over the future. Esteemed anthropological texts accentuate how control is sought by *calculation and regulation* of danger. My social psychological stance accentuates the seeking out of control via *representation*. When a defensive prism has been established, anxiety is not raised by even a barrage of dangers. I integrate strands of social representations and psycho-dynamic theory to forge a framework for understanding social representations of risks which leave people with a strong sense of invulnerability.

'Natural' and technological disasters continue to increase in both frequency and severity (Oliver-Smith, 1996). Disasters form an ongoing backdrop to human existence. The Red Cross's annual list of the world's worst non-conflict disasters in the past few years includes meningitis, cholera and malaria epidemics, as well as typhoons, floods, cyclones and storms. Earthquakes, volcanoes and hurricanes have also loomed large. Such disasters affect millions of people. Each phase in history throws up a plethora of disasters. The rapid increase in population size, use of advanced technology and increased air-travel have all contributed to the massive scale of contemporary disasters at a material level. In addition, the mass mediation of local disasters globally has contributed to the sense of being surrounded by a plethora of mass crises. In line with the Western desire to seize control, these factors prompted the United Nations to declare the 1990s the International Decade for Natural Disaster Reduction.

It is timely to draw together common threads in the analysis of responses to risk across the social sciences. Material vulnerability to different types of disasters depends upon multiple factors including social, political and economic structures (Porto and Defreitas, 1996). However, my key concern is with a framework for understanding how thinking processes operate in the face of this vulnerability. Wynne

(1996) favours transferring the focus from the 'real' nature of risk – which he construes as the focus in the accounts of Beck and Giddens – to the cultural and social dimensions that surround risk. I support this orientation: material circumstances pose risks, but it is the expert and lay conceptions of these circumstances that constitute what is understood to be threatening. It is for this reason that I dwell on neither the 'real' threat posed, nor the 'biased' or 'unrealistic' thinking which arises, in relation to such threats. Rather, the focus is upon meanings made of what come to be represented as material threats. The challenge is to find patterns of psychic response common to all risks, with an eye to how changes in these responses may come about.

NOTES

1 The terms potential disaster, potential crisis, imminent danger and risk are used interchangeably in this book, since risk is defined as 'danger from future damage' (Douglas, 1992).

2 This World Health Organisation position paper on health risks states that when communities decide which risks to focus on, statistical issues must be considered: common problems must be given more priority than more rare problems, problems with more serious outcomes must be given more priority than those with less serious outcomes, easily preventable problems must be given priority over those more difficult to prevent, and those with frequency increasing must be given more priority than those with static or declining frequencies.

3 The focus of the book is on early reactions to potential dangers which come to the person's awareness, often via the mass media or people discussing the content of the mass media. Therefore, I do not discuss the effects of personal experiences of the threat, or personal contact with those who have already been affected.

4 I utilise the 'not me – others' concept as a shorthand for the set of concepts: 'not me', 'not my group', 'others are to blame'.

5 Within much of the health literature 'illness' refers to the physical and mental states which are deemed pathological in Western culture, whereas 'disease' refers to the social construction which provides a framework within which to understand illness. I generally use the term illness, but since I attempt to reconcile the material and social constructionist bases of risks (see chapter 2), this encompasses both facets.

6 Gilman does not see this as exclusively a Western attribute but tends to focus on the West. Crawford (1994) assumes that Gilman sees projection of vulnerability onto others as a universal, human process.

7 One example of this, offered by Gilman (1985b), is that the image of the diseased person as ugly has been challenged in contemporary AIDS campaigns which generally depict erotic images. This relates, among other forces, to the opposition, by the gay pride movement of the 1960s, to images of the 'pathologised homosexual'.

2   Human responses to risks: 'not me', 'the other is to blame'

How are outsiders represented in societies? This question must be addressed prior to exploration of the representations of 'the other' which arise at times of imminent danger. Regard for 'the other' is intricately connected with the 'not me', 'not my group' response. In this chapter I demonstrate that people establish a positive sense of identity by way of the juxtaposition between what can comfortably be associated with 'others' and elements with which 'self' seeks to affiliate.

The 'not me – other' response

Regard for 'the other' in an ongoing sense

Before exploring the association between 'otherness' and moments of potential disaster, it is important to decipher how 'the other' is regarded in an ongoing sense in society. The concept 'the other' is very widely used in cultural theory.[1] The word 'other' generally includes those outside of, and implicitly subordinate to, the dominant group. According to Said (1978), a distinctive aspect of being 'other' is that one is the object of someone else's fantasies, but not a subject with agency and voice. This can be illustrated by his claims concerning 'the Orient'. The Orient was an entity constructed by European culture. During the post-Enlightenment period a set of political, sociological, military, ideological and scientific discourses established 'the Orient'. Members of 'the Orient' did not speak of themselves. They did not represent their own emotions or history. Rather, the Orient was filtered through the lens of European culture. This lens diminished the status of 'Orientals'. European culture gained strength and identity by contrasting itself to the Orient in a manner that allowed it to appear superior.

This highlights a crucial aspect of how people forge their identities. Identity is constructed not only by what people affiliate with, but by *comparison* to other groups. Gaining a positive sense of identity through comparison with negatively valued groups is common in modern and

18

'primitive' societies alike, according to Said (1978). A fifth century BC Athenian was as likely to gain a sense of identity from being a non-Barbarian, as from positively feeling like an Athenian. In a similar line of reasoning, Stallybrass and White (1986) show that the bourgeois person continually defined the self through the exclusion of what was marked out as 'low', be it dirty, repulsive, noisy or contaminating. This act of exclusion was constitutive of identity. This theme crops up again in McCulloch's (1995) analysis of the work of psychiatrists in Africa in the first sixty years of the twentieth century. The written work of these men described the 'African' in terms of everything that the 'European' was not. Africans emerged from these writings as savage, lazy, violent and sexually promiscuous, the very antithesis of Europeans with their order, reason, moral standards, discipline, sexual continence, self-control and altruism. McCulloch points out that this finding resonates with earlier writings on race, with their emphasis on the virtues of white people and the vices of black people.

A number of theorists have identified a *specific pattern* that is evident in Western understanding of 'others'. The set of comparisons between Westerners and non-Westerners contains a vision of 'the other' in terms of a vivid collection of images. First and foremost, 'the other' is considered to be different from the European. More particularly, 'the other' is viewed in terms of two extremes: highly debased and also extremely admirable and enviable. These seemingly opposite currents of the representation are intertwined. Cultural theorists (e.g. Said, 1978; Hall, 1991) map the specific content of the debased and admiring representations that dominant groups have of 'the other'. In particular, those who are from non-hegemonic groups are invested with excessive sexuality, emotionality and spirituality. People who have not kept pace with the Western notions of progress are seen to possess Black Magic, primitive mentality, animism and animal eroticism (Fanon, 1992). They are imbued with both supernatural and instinctual qualities. They are lauded for their artistic, spiritual and erotic prowess. Such abilities evoke admiration. These facets of human experience are kept underground, surrounded by taboo, in the rational climate of Western culture. Simultaneous to admiring these qualities, Western societies are also threatened by them. These attributes challenge the omnipotence attributed to science and to rationality, by demonstrating the coexistence of other belief systems and values. Their very presence challenges the status quo, evoking fear in relation to the havoc they may wreak in the existing order. Comparisons in which non-Western cultures emerge as inferior in terms of the core values of the West may be a reaction to this threat. They are part of the 'identity work' (Crawford, 1994) carried out by Westerners. Characteristics which are admired for their exoticism simultaneously threaten the sense of order enshrined in Western law, intellect and morality.

Convincing historical evidence for the mixture of admiration and debasement of the other is provided by Young's (1995) analysis of representations of black people in the West. A key focus is on the work of the influential nineteenth-century scholar Gobineau (1856). He postulated that races had their own characteristics as shown in the table.

Characteristics of the races according to Gobineau (1856)[2]

	Black races	Yellow races	White races
Intellect	Feeble	Mediocre	Vigorous
Animal propensities	Very strong	Moderate	Strong
Moral manifestations	Partially latent	Comparatively developed	Highly cultivated

Gobineau's typology is believed to have had a major impact on Hitler's racial theories. The 'white' races are perceived to be highly developed intellectually and morally. As one moves towards the more 'black' racial pole, the focus is on powerful, animalistic properties, often affiliated with an overdeveloped sexuality. Their strong animal propensities have the consequence that, within the nineteenth-century literature, black people are affiliated with 'nature', while culture and civilisation become properties exclusive to white people.

Sexual aspersions form a particularly salient feature in the degrading representations which Westerners hold of 'the other' in an enduring sense. In nineteenth-century academic works there is a common predilection for expressing racist views via mention of sexuality (Young, 1995). Non-Europeans are often represented as having excessive and illicit sex. This includes mixed race liaisons and bestiality. An authoritative work on the history of Jamaica in the nineteenth century, for example, characterised Jamaican women as 'libidinous and shameless as monkeys, or baboons' and claimed that these animals were frequently admitted to the women's embrace (Young, 1995). The decline of Western civilisation is imagined to follow from such unions. Yet alongside a judgement of these acts as repugnant, there is emphasis on the striking sexual charm and beauty of women who are mixtures of white and black races. Interestingly, Watney (1989) has shown that Africans and 'perverts' were constructed in a similar way in nineteenth-century taxonomies. There is:

a close parallel between anthropological attention to African sexuality, illustrated in the lantern light of eugenic theory, and the equally spectacular inventory of 'the perversions' so painstakingly catalogued by the early sexologists. Blacks and 'perverts' alike were held to share the characteristics of unbridled sexual rapacity and low cunning. (Watney, 1989: 95).

A further aspect of the entwined negative–positive representation of 'others' was the very pleasure derived from witnessing their 'perversion'. At the same time as distancing themselves from the acts of black people and 'perverts', Westerners were eager to classify, to explain and to represent such acts. In nineteenth-century Western Europe black women, in particular, were represented in terms of hypersexuality and the exotic. They were widely perceived to possess both a 'primitive' sexual appetite and the external signs of this: 'primitive' genitalia. Black women were imagined to copulate with apes, as a further equation between them and the animal universe. Diagrams and exhibits of the genitals of Hottentot women were on show in European museums in the nineteenth century.[3] The difference between their genitals and those of Western women was used to indicate that they were a lower species. They were not only more 'primitive' but also more sexual. At the same time as being disparaged as lowly creatures, Hottentot women were depicted as highly sexual objects in the art of the day (Gilman, 1992). Desire, expressed in the form of voyeurism, was also reflected in the incarceration of people from Africa in the zoos of Germany, Austria and Budapest, prior to the First World War (Gilman, 1985a). The representation of 'the other' was constituted by both the desirable and the 'less than civilised' aspects of black people in general, and black women in particular. Western desire was stoked, levels of repugnance were raised, by the voyeuristic gaze into the 'exotic' practices of out-groups.

The dual workings of disgust and desire are illuminated by Stallybrass and White (1986). They state that elements of experience that are subordinated in a society become central in the formation of desire. Components of a culture that are socially peripheral are symbolically central. Cultures think about themselves in terms of hierarchies in which some elements are 'high' and others 'low'. Bourgeois culture represents its 'low' other in terms of disgust, fear and desire:

disgust always bears the imprint of desire. These low domains, apparently expelled as 'Other', return as the object of nostalgia, longing and fascination. The forest, the fair, the theatre, the slum, the circus, the seaside-resort, the 'savage': all these, placed at the outer limit of civil life, become symbolic contents of bourgeois desire. (Stallybrass and White, 1986: 191).

This double impulse is interesting in terms of the development of democracy. Bourgeois democracy emerged with a class which was progressive in its political ideals but had elitism encoded in its manners, morals, tastes and bodily practices. Engraved in the bourgeois identity were the marks of being different and superior.

I have focused on the representation of debased-desired out-groups in nineteenth-century thought. Yet this representation predates this period, stretching way back in time. For example, when they were in power, the Romans regarded the early Christians as erotically perverse as a consequence of their rendering of rituals such as the Agape and the Bacchanalia. Excessive eating and drinking were inherent to the Christian Agape, in which baptised Christians feasted communally, with the intention of affirming Christian fellowship. The Romans represented this in light of their own Bacchanalia or nocturnal orgies. Romans interpreted these activities in terms of erotic debauches, cannibalism and infanticide. Medieval Christendom revived these Roman tales and applied them to religious out-groups: 'Again and again, over a period of centuries, heretical sects were accused of holding promiscuous orgies in the dark . . . of worshipping the devil' (Cohn, 1976: 54). Throughout history fantasies about the rituals of out-groups have been used to denigrate them, often via imbuing their practices with sexual, animalistic connotations.

The regard for 'the other' at times of crisis

Having focused on regard for 'the other' in an ongoing sense, I turn to the impact that crises have on these representations, according to social scientific writings. A core claim is that the tendency to infuse others with unwanted parts of the dominant culture becomes magnified in representations which flourish at times of crisis. Nazi texts provide a useful starting point for uniting work on 'the other' and that on crisis. Against a backdrop of a mounting economic crisis, the Nazi texts which dominated German thinking between 1933 and 1945 describe Jewish people, whom the Nazis sought to blame for the crisis, as 'vermin', 'bacteria', 'pests' and 'international maggots', and also as 'satanic', 'devils' and 'demons' (Bar-Tal, 1990). Degradation of Jews is accomplished by way of dehumanisation. This involves drawing on categories of non-human, negatively valued creatures. The 'other' is represented as evil either via a link to contaminating insects, or to supernatural creatures. In the face of a highly threatening situation, which laid German people open to feelings of weakness and vulnerability, a debased 'other' provided a punch-bag, a repository for blame. If human groups can be construed as lower forms of life, the respect demanded by Western culture in relation to humans can be disregarded. A key feature of the Nazi texts was emphasis of the lascivious nature of Jewish women, associating 'the other' with animal-like instincts, and with sexuality. Once debased by being associated with animals, the out-group becomes imbued with sexual and instinctual powers.

In periods of crisis, when anxiety is raised, the out-group moves from being represented as mildly threatening, a challenge to the core values of the society, to being seen as the purveyor of chaos, a cat among the pigeons. While 'the other' is defined in terms of difference and inferiority in relation to normative values in an ongoing sense, the representations that arise at times of crisis intensify this distinction. They reflect a very powerful division between a decorous, righteous 'us' and a disruptive, transgressive 'them' (Douglas, 1966). Communities have an impetus to maintain the safety and comfort of the decorous members. This is achieved by way of vivid representations which undermine outsiders by construing their practices as deviant. The decorum of 'us' is sustained through imbuing others with properties which fall outside of what is valued in the society.

The 'other' is not only represented as a threat in that it embodies that which must be kept at bay symbolically if the society is to feel safe. As a consequence of being a symbolic repository for that which societies, cultures and groups want to expel, 'the other' comes to be seen as a material threat. The disdain with which the behaviour of 'the other' is regarded is heightened by the physical threat which outsiders are imagined to pose to mainstream society. In the early years of the AIDS crisis, for example, Altman (1986) noted that most people's contact with the syndrome was linked to the fear of contagion, rather than to any direct experience of illness. Undoubtably this is true of other epidemics which have taken hold in this age, an age in which the mass media provide experience of a far greater range of mass crises than are locally prevalent. AIDS was conceptualised in the early media as an illness that leaked from an infected homosexual source to the rest of the world (Watney, 1987). The responses to many crises relate to the potential perforation of the boundaries between 'us' and 'them', to invasion of the equilibrium by viruses, radiation, genetically engineered products and so on. Yet Douglas (1966) singles out sexually related danger as particularly likely to evoke fears of invasion and pollution. Sexual relations, in themselves, involve the perforation of boundaries between bodies. The penetration of orifices and mixing of bodily substances are synonymous with processes of infection. A fear of infection intensifies the need to draw a distinction between 'us' and 'them'. This is particularly marked in responses to epidemics, and magnified in relation to those represented as sexually transmitted, though by no means exclusive to this type of mass crisis.

The link between disaster and sexuality stretches back way beyond modernity. It is a strong theme in the Bible. Natural catastrophes including mass diseases, floods and famines continue to be filtered through the moral vision of the Old Testament (Gilbert and Barkun, 1981). The salience of the ongoing link between sin, particularly sexually related sin, and disaster must be emphasised. The connection to sin, the connection to punishment from God, still influences current reactions to mass crises. Before scientists became the chief purveyors of information about risks, it was standard practice for representatives of religious establishments to explain catastrophes in terms of the sinfulness of society. God's law was often assumed to have been violated, and violations were often presumed to be of a sexual nature. For earthquakes and volcanoes, for example, God was punishing Sodom and Gomorrah for licentiousness. Interestingly, Gilbert and Barkun (1981) suggest that the growth of cities in the eighteenth century in the West brought the link between disaster, sin and sexuality into sharper focus. Sin became linked with urban centres, in the way that evil had been coupled with Sodom and Gomorrah. Eighteenth-century London, for example, was seen as a centre of licentious behaviours, such as homosexuality. Clergymen explained the two London earthquakes of the 1750s in terms of moral decay. The link between sodomy and urban catastrophe, which has been presented as a powerful theme in representation of AIDS, with its links to bathhouse culture, stretches way back. While the belief that God causes disasters to punish people for sins persists from early Christian times, self-inflicted misfortune is increasingly implicated in disasters, especially epidemics.

Control, as opposed to indulgence, is a core norm in Western society. Western cultures have developed a fear and fascination regarding 'the other', who is believed to take on the characteristics antithetical to the self-control, self-denial and self-discipline which Westerners value (Crawford, 1994). The drug user, the alcoholic, the smoker, the person with AIDS, all are associated with excess, addiction, a loss of these cherished qualities. People acting in a manner deemed to be out of control present a major threat to the Protestant ethic of moderation. Protestantism has helped to create a self preoccupied with discipline. Calvinism, in particular, demonstrates a horror of disorder. A secular push towards civility has worked alongside this religious force in the West. Crawford proposes that health is laden with metaphors about what it means to be a responsible, respectable and inherently good citizen. He puts forward a powerful argument that health, which he goes as far as to call the emblem of modern, Western identity, has become a metaphor for self-control, self-discipline, self-denial and will power.

Interestingly, Crawford proposes that in Western culture the self is not just associated with control but with a release from it. Pleasures, desires, gratification and play are intrinsic aspects of consumer culture. Health has become the arena through which the tension between self-control and the very release from it plays out. However, rather than holding these two antithetical components together, the culture expunges its association with the uncontrolled aspects – such as addictions – linking them with disparaged 'others'. These 'others' are blamed for bringing their ill health upon themselves, and held outside of the culture symbolically, so that the self cannot be morally infected.

Representations of the risks posed by epidemics, in particular, have been closely scrutinised for their blaming aspersions. Research on responses to epidemics conducted from a variety of methodological, disciplinary and cultural standpoints has indicated that people dissociate themselves from epidemics and locate them with certain 'others'. The response to syphilis when it began its sweep through Europe in the fifteenth century provides the now classic example of the 'not me – others', response: 'It was the "French pox" to the English, *morbus Germanicus* to the Parisians, the Naples sickness to the Florentines, the Chinese disease to the Japanese' (Sontag, 1989:47). Factors involved in this pattern of naming syphilis are similar to those found in relation to other epidemics.

An external origin and source are implicated in the names given to syphilis. Yet to be external, to be outside of a society one need not reside on foreign soil. Out-groups within each society, and their practices, have also been linked to the genesis of epidemics. In addition to the association with foreigners, nineteenth-century Western cultures linked syphilis with black women and with prostitutes, as well as with unbridled sexual practices (Gilman, 1992). The same pattern of representation can be found in relation to a large number of epidemics. Cholera was termed 'Asiatic Cholera' in the first of the large-scale epidemics in Britain in 1832. It was connected with dirt and with excessive drink and passion. The middle and upper classes had an image of the victims as lower-class, filthy, poor and drunken (Morris, 1976). In the United States poliomyelitis, often assumed to be a mass, incurable illness which did not elicit a link to an outsider status (due to its association with children), was, in fact, associated with Jewish and Italian immigrants and with dirty practices, prior to the popularisation of Franklin D. Roosevelt's paralysis from it in 1921 (Rogers, 1992). Similarly, typhus was imagined to be brought into Britain in 1847 by refugees from the Irish famine (Morris, 1976). Finally, leprosy first came to international public notice when it was reported to be spreading in Hawaii, in the 1960s (Gussow, 1989). Western fears of 'Oriental leprosy' fed calls for exclusion of those thought to be the carriers of leprosy – Chinese people – from centres of Western civilisation.

Mass, incurable illnesses, from syphilis to cholera, from the Black Death to leprosy, have been linked to 'the other' both historically and cross-culturally. The 'other' in these and further writings on threat comprises three interrelated phenomena: foreign nations, out-groups within a society and practices which are construed as alien within the prevailing norms of the culture. The practices construed as deviant are those associated with excess, a lack of control and self-indulgence. The table provides an overview of how Anglo-culture has represented various epidemics.

Epidemic	Foreigner	Out-group	Alien practice
Leprosy (Gussow, 1989)	Orientals	Chinese living outside of China	Sex, dirt
Syphilis (Sontag, 1989; Gilman, 1992)	French pox (Sontag, 1989)	Prostitutes, black women (Gilman, 1992)	Promiscuity (Sontag, 1989; Gilman, 1992)
Cholera (Morris, 1976)	Asia	The poor	Excessive drinking and passion
Typhus (Morris, 1976)	Irish	The poor	Dirt

Historical work on health and illness reveals that a variant of the ethic of moderation stretches way back in time in the West. The central texts used by English medics at the time of the fifteenth-century bubonic plague, for example, suggested a temperate lifestyle to avoid infection, including avoidance of lust with women, who were associated with putrification (Gottfried, 1978). Gottfried suggests that advocation of an ethic of moderation has been in existence since Aristotelian times.

Even though members of populations have often believed that mass crises are forms of punishment, they have always seized certain forms of control when faced with imminent danger. One form of control, to which I pay greatest attention in this book, is to set up representations that declare which groups and practices pollute the order and decorum of the community. Such representations can lead to the desire for the elimination of this polluting force. Scapegoating is a way of ridding a community of the impure elements, those represented as the source of the chaos. The concept of scapegoating implies that one organism, totally innocent of causing the event for which it is being blamed, is sacrificed for the purification of others (Douglas, 1995). The prototypical act which aims to restore order utilises scapegoats for the ritual transfer of evil from inside to outside the community. In the Bible, a goat was forced to leave the boundaries of the community in order to ameliorate the community's problems. The humans chosen to fulfil this role are those who are different or deficient, relative to the norm. They are represented as those who contravene the beliefs and rules of behaviour, as well as the laws of 'nature'. Accounts of crises are shot through with accusations levelled at people who have tampered with the balance of either society or of 'nature'. These accusations may precipitate punitive actions.

I have explored the ongoing debasement of 'others' in Western societies, which becomes magnified at times of crisis. At such times 'others' carry what societies want to distance themselves from in an effort to sustain a sense of orderliness. 'Others' are denounced for having contributed to the crisis, for polluting the 'general public'. A variant of 'the other' as an inadvertent polluter is the idea that others set out, maliciously, to contaminate certain groups. Particular groups are perceived to have actively conspired to infect other groups, rather than having unwittingly upset the balance of 'nature' or of the norms in a given society. Theories of conspiracy, in particular, posit that a group actively plots to bring about a crisis in a society to achieve a specific end. In contemporary crises, it is those who are regarded as 'other' within mainstream norms who often adopt such theories. Precisely those who have been accused of introducing HIV/AIDS to the Western world, for example, have been the chief purveyors of conspiracy theories. Early on in the crisis, Western gay and African publications forged their own links between 'the other' and threat: the epidemic was seen as a conspiracy by Western scientists and policy-makers to attack out-groups. In terms of the AIDS pandemic, conspiracy theories have been the 'rhetorical defence' (Farmer, 1992:247) of groups in society who lack power.

Highlighting the group-specific explanations of crises is crucial in that it signals that differing responses arise in different sectors of a society. Like dominant groups, non-hegemonic groups have 'others' whom they link to threat. The supposition that powerful groups – often encompassed in the notion of 'Westerners' by cultural theorists – have exceptional patterns of thought concerning the non-powerful, overlooks the more widespread nature of this configuration. Scrutiny of how non-powerful groups regard their 'other' is useful in demonstrating that self – other relations contain universal aspects which are not necessarily related to Western ideological issues, as is suggested in much cultural theory.

The point made by Said (1978), in order to elucidate the hegemony of the Western viewpoint, is that the very presence of a 'field' or discipline termed Orientalism, with no corresponding 'Occidentalism' in 'Oriental' countries, suggests the relative strength of the Orient as opposed to the Occident. Said's deduction, that the West saw the Orient in terms of degrading and admiring representations, is drawn from his distillation of the ideas put forward in the tens of thousands of Western books written about the Orient between 1800 and 1950. There is no equivalent Oriental writing about the West, in either volume or coherence of themes. I would like to throw light on this claim, by touching upon evidence of how Africans represent 'others' when they explain the source of illnesses. I expand upon this investigation in chapter 3. The key issue is to direct attention to whether non-Westerners have similar or different patterns of representations to those of Westerners, at times of crisis.

Ngubane's (1977) anthropological work on Zulu people's ideas concerning physical and mental illness provides an illuminating account of how 'the alien' or 'the other' is given a role in the genesis of these illnesses. The Zulu belief is that when physical and mental illness strike, this is the result of intruding spirits. Evil spirits are spirits of aliens. Two forms of possession by evil spirits relate to the intrusion by alien people into Zulu culture. One form, *indiki*, occurs due to violation of principles of patrilineage, often believed to occur when non-Zulu men have sexual relationships with Zulu women. Another form of spirit possession is *ufufunyane*: thousands of spirits of various races are believed to possess a person. Violent, hysterical and suicidal behaviour are indications of this form of possession. Physical and mental illness result from spirit possession; spirits possess people because the balance of the community has been violated in some way. As in the West, when order has been overturned, a set of explanations arise involving an intrusive 'other'. 'The other' pollutes an otherwise balanced community.

'The other' in Ngubane's work on Zulus is the foreigner. In further work on African representations of epidemic illness, it is embodied in women. For the Tswana of Botswana, the spread of disease is associated with pollution. This originates in women's bodies and transmits to men via sexual relationships which occur when women are not ritually pure (i.e. post-partum and after widowhood) (Goldin, 1994). The link between disease and foreignness is complex in African culture. Goldin states that sexually transmitted diseases are interpreted as indigenous in origin by a number of African societies. Yet illnesses are understood to be triggered by supernatural forces acting in response to transgressions of rules of sexual behaviour. Among these contraventions is having sex with foreigners.

Empirically grounded research in different cultures, at least in the case of illness, suggests a degree of similarity between Westerners and non-Westerners in the explanations that arise at times of crisis. Just as Westerners linked syphilis with various 'others' so, in Tahiti, syphilis was known as 'English disease' (Davenport-Hines, 1990). Even though Western writings on non-Westerners far outnumber non-Western writings involving Westerners, the symmetry in the literature that exists is fascinating. It corroborates Douglas' (1992) contention that there is a continuity rather than a disjunction between Western and non-Western responses to crises. The need for control lies at their root, and the strict divisions between decorum and transgression are therefore present in both types of societies. There is an abiding human response to danger, to crises, which the modern age has not impacted upon (Douglas, 1966; Douglas and Wildawsky, 1983). This is highly significant in that it suggests that humans the world over react similarly, psychically, to crises. This indicates that the framework chosen to explain the response to crisis needs to be concerned with universal, subjective responses. I draw on the psycho-dynamic tradition to develop this aspect of the framework, while highlighting socio-cultural differences in the representations of crises.

Any claim that all groups have 'others' whom they blame in times of crisis needs to be tempered by reference to power differences in societies. We cannot overlook the hegemonic position of Western culture worldwide. Western representations of AIDS, to take but one example, have far wider currency throughout the world than non-Western representations do, due to the universally dominant position held by the Western mass media and by Western science itself. Dominant groups exert their control by controlling the process of representation; some representations gain greater currency than others on the world stage. There is a silencing of certain voices, while others are more pronounced. Even though there is a tendency among all groups to say 'not me – others are to blame' at times of crisis, the shape of such representations evolves within an ideological climate in which certain and not other practices and thoughts are deemed acceptable. However, it is important not to lose sight of the symmetry inherent in perceiving the 'other' at times of crisis. The 'other' forms a potential repository of blame among hegemonic and non-hegemonic group members alike.

The 'not me' response to potential disasters

I have focused on the way in which 'the other' becomes particularly vilified at times of crisis. It is chiefly cultural theorists, historians and anthropologists who have deduced this link. A complementary set of links has been made by psychologists. Their work plays up the individual, rather than community and cultural, aspects of the response to risks. It emphasises the personal sense of invulnerability – 'it won't happen to me' – rather than how others are regarded at times of crisis. However, the 'not me' and 'others are to blame' responses are different sides of the same coin. Both are germane in the construction of a positive sense of identity. The space of the self is kept pure of associations with misfortune, and it is 'the other' who becomes linked to such events.

I shall outline the data presented in three psychological collections on responses to potential disasters. These data augment major themes that arise from the other social sciences: that control lies at the heart of responses to potential disasters and that the 'not me' response is prevalent among people from various cultures. They also show that the patterns of response to epidemic and economic crises, which I have mentioned, generalise to industrial accidents, to nuclear fall-out and to wars.

Mearns and Flin's (1996) 'Risk perception in hazardous industries' amalgamates data on the perception of risk in industries chosen on the basis that they have the highest fatal and non-fatal injury rates of all industries. They show that data from a number of European countries reveal an underestimation of risk by workers. In a Swedish study of nuclear power plant workers (Sjoberg and Drottz-Sjoberg, 1991) the workers judge their job-related radiation risks to be lower than risks which accrue from smoking, aircraft accidents and downhill skiing. This is an incorrect reading of the relative riskiness of the various activities, if one compares the known probabilities and the workers' judgements. An additional 'perceptual error' manifests: workers who have the least knowledge about the risks of radiation perceive the greatest risk. With increased knowledge, the perception of risk diminishes. The supposition that people read their risks in a 'biased' way is echoed in Zimolong's (1985) study of German construction workers. In familiar situations at work, which contain a high risk, risk is underestimated as compared with unknown situations which contain similar levels of risk. Interestingly, both knowledge about, and familiarity with, the risky situation may militate against a cautious outlook. Mearns and Flin's (1996) overview shows that high levels of familiarity with work tasks play a role in the underestimation of the risks they pose. In addition, workers who perceive themselves to be most in control of a task tend to underestimate their risks, probably because they imagine that their mastery of the situation actually reduces the risk. A strong sense of control and high levels of knowledge may be linked. They militate against caution in potentially risky situations.

In *Individual and community responses to trauma and disaster*, Ursano, *et al.* (1994) integrate disaster, war and other trauma studies. While the Mearns and Flin (1996) collection was concerned with the mismatch between 'risk as subjectively perceived' and 'risk as objectively measured', their emphasis is upon the emotionally and socially based processes activated by potential crises. The studies in this anthology indicate that disasters stir terror, generally by exposing people to the potential of death. The human way of returning to a state of functioning, in the face of disaster, is by making meaning, making structure of terror and chaos. People are motivated to feel safe, to experience the environment as stable and predictable. However, humans do not pursue this goal on an individual basis, according to Holloway and Fullerton (1994). Rather, a shared set of meanings of the event is established by groups, reflected in their shared beliefs and enshrined in the rituals and symbols which organise an event. Fairy tales are particularly good examples of shared sets of meanings which lie at the root of many people's understanding and experience of terror. The terror of a loss of safety and of vulnerability are often at the root of such tales. Fairy tales show that although evil and terror exist, they can be controlled: in stories ranging from 'Jack and the Bean Stalk' to 'Hansel and Gretel' children are taught that terror is a manageable part of the world (Bettleheim, 1977). Children's predilection to fairy tales is linked with the sense of mastery over terror that they provide. The fairy tale, rather than an adult symbolisation of terror, forms the strongest example in the Ursano *et al.* (1994) collection. Despite the differences between the approach of this compilation, and that of Mearns and Flin (1996), both cast light on the exaggeration of the sense of control, when people evaluate potential risks.

The core findings of the older literature on disaster contain similar elements to the more contemporary studies. *Man and society in disaster* (Baker and Chapman, 1962) is an anthology written to provide the US government with adequate theories to help it in its dealings with nuclear attacks. It is rooted in the disaster research of its time. A key finding is that the great majority of the public in the United States think that the country would be attacked in the event of a further war. Yet half the population feel that they do not need to pay attention to civil defence because they can discount any danger to themselves (Withey, 1962). One explanation of this finding is that people overestimate the probability that good events will affect them and underestimate their probability of being affected by bad events (Chapman, 1962). This is achieved by downplaying the threatening cues: when alerted to disasters people feel that they will not happen or, if they do, that they are unlikely to be as bad as predicted. Some justify this by way of a perception of their own locale as intrinsically 'safe' while others feel that the relevant physical defences will be strong enough to ward off an attacker (Withey, 1962). Again a sense of control over the disaster features as a central variable in the 'it won't happen to me' response. Furthermore, this anthology emphasises the role of a sense of personal immunity and stability in the face of potential crises. When confronted with the possibility of social fragmentation, as occurs when people are faced with disasters, every effort is made to maintain a sense of immunity to the crisis. This serves to maintain a sense of stability for the psyche. Defence by way of denial occurs.

The primarily empirically based literature (cited above) offers evidence of the existence of, and some of the forces at work in, the 'not me' phenomenon. While all of this work highlights the importance of maintaining a sense of control, the early work places greater emphasis upon the unconscious defensiveness which is activated by potential disasters. The assumption is made that each individual brings the denial defence into play. This is a very different supposition from that of perceptual 'error' made by the most recent anthology. These differences are teased out in chapter 4.

A material basis for the 'not me – others' response?

To what extent do the material causes of a crisis play a role in the representations that surround it? If one adheres to the notion of scapegoating, people who are totally innocent of causing disasters are blamed in order to purify the community. My major contention is similar in that 'others' are implicated in crises for reasons which lie with the accusers rather than the accused. This suggests that the accused are slates for projection, without any material connection to the crisis. What if features of 'the other's' lifestyle or identity are indeed associated with the genesis of the crisis in question? What if scapegoating involves parties who *are* connected to the event for which they are blamed in a material sense?

A number of the researchers who tracked the epidemic illnesses which I have addressed certainly believe that these epidemics were accurately associated with outsider identities and practices. According to Morris (1976) the nineteenth-century cholera epidemics came from Bengal and only 10 per cent of its victims (in a UK group studied in 1932) were middle class, with the rest being lower class. Morris also states that the nineteenth-century typhus epidemic came to Britain via refugees from the Irish famine. Other historians make similar assumptions. Davenport-

Hines (1990) states that syphilis was brought back to Europe and the Orient from the Americas by Columbus in 1493. A further theory posits that the syphilis of the fifteenth- and sixteenth-century European epidemic was an African disease imported by the slaves of West and North Africa to the Iberian peninsula (Morton, 1971). So these authors' accounts support the claim that representations of cholera, typhus and syphilis in terms of 'other' identities are rooted in material 'facts'.

This is among the more interesting and difficult elements of a discussion of representations of 'the other'. A useful starting point is to acknowledge that even the most empirically 'objective' of observations must be interpreted by a researcher and this subjects the results to historical and cultural influences. All 'facts' are refracted through the lens of the individual or institution that proclaims them. Texts from the developing world demonstrate that the identity of the researcher shapes the explanation offered for a crisis. For example, they propose diametrically opposite theories of the origin of syphilis to those accepted as 'true' in the West. Syphilis, for example, is imagined to have been brought to the underdeveloped world by way of slave-traders, missionaries, colonisers and Western travellers (Trevisan, 1986). Rosebury (1972: 49) points out that 'We are not likely ever to know beyond a doubt how syphilis began, or when. But the question continues to be asked, and answered'. The types of questions asked and the variety of answers given attest to the identity-protective character of the inquiry and the conclusions it draws, even at its most scientific. Certainly when the shock of potential disaster is initially assimilated, the 'not me – others' explanation appears, irrespective of a grounding in material 'realities'. This applies not just to lay and mass mediated explanations, but also to the avenues initially explored by scientists, who are deemed the experts in interpreting contemporary disasters. This is demonstrated in chapter 3.

Traditionally, that which science names is deemed to be 'fact' or 'material reality' while the mass media and lay thinking are believed to draw on the more mythical elements of knowledge (Comaroff, 1982), entering the fantastical with greater ease and relish. However, many empirical studies (e.g. Bloor, 1976; Latour and Woolgar, 1979; Collins, 1985) show that scientific 'facts' are produced in a manner akin to the production of knowledge in other spheres. In a line of thought conceived by Lévi-Strauss, anthropologists and sociologists suggest that while modern science and 'myth' appear to be fundamentally different, both are attempts to order the chaos in the perceived relation of men to nature. The claim that I develop throughout this book is that this chaos is ordered, initially, by scientists, journalists and lay people alike, by means of self-protective representations. The fundamental dynamic, when faced with a crisis, is to form representations which protect the positive identity of the in-group. Linking epidemics with out-groups, foreigners and 'perverse' practices serves this function. Since it is firmly established that group identity forms a component of self-identity (Tajfel and Turner, 1979), the process of linking epidemics with 'the other' sustains a positive self-identity. The motivation to forge a positive sense of identity explains why groups, including scientists, ascribe to representations in accordance with the identities which require protection. Such representations localise the crisis in others as a means of ridding the self from fears of being afflicted. This idea, which draws heavily upon Melanie Klein's clinically based ideas, and is widely associated with the cultural historian Sander Gilman's (1985a) work, finds resonance in many insights concerning the mechanisms of constructing identity. Stallybrass and White's (1986) ideas about the bourgeois person constructing a positive sense of cultural identity by expelling that which is marked out as 'low' augments this idea, as does Said's (1978) claim that Europeans gained a superior sense of their identity through comparison with others who they marked out as inferior in terms of the traits valued by Europeans.

A positive sense of self-identity is not equally accessible for every member of society. The interests of the dominant groups in a society become seamlessly incorporated into the set of tacit assumptions concerning what the 'material facts' are in a society (see Comaroff, 1982). Certain interests shape what come to be viewed as 'material facts'. Social interests are imbibed by lay people while they witness the media representing scientific 'facts'. Depending upon where the individual thinker is positioned, this ideological level may make it difficult for a positive sense of identity to be attained. The relative access to a positive sense of identity by a healthy person, as opposed to a person with AIDS, who may hold a spoiled identity as a consequence of the stigma faced, speaks to this disparity.

In chapter 3 I add weight to these claims via exploration of the workings of scientific and lay responses to the AIDS epidemic, which has had a massive universal impact on both the sexual mores of the late twentieth century and on the academic commentary on risk. I have argued that crises get refracted through a lens in which group and self-identity are germane, as are the interests of the dominant groups. However, it is important at least to consider whether an epidemic such as AIDS could have been consistently linked to homosexual practices such as anal sex, in the West, if this material practice had played no role whatsoever in the spread of HIV. Crises do not tolerate all interpretations – they are not completely open to any conceivable representation.

If we are to gain a fuller understanding of responses to crises we need to recognise that the material practises which are implicated and which may, indeed, be materially linked to the crisis, exist outside of the realm of representation. However, as soon as they are represented they are used towards certain ends. Dehumanisation, expressed in accusations of animal-like (avaricious, promiscuous, bestial) sexuality, is certainly a way in which dominant groups, faced with crises, have denunciated out-groups throughout history. Insinuation of excessive indulgence of various types has been used to demarcate that which lies outside of the acceptable bounds of behaviour, and is therefore deserving of retribution.

By focusing upon representations I am in no way denying the material facets of risks which often involve a threat to the bodies of individuals at a physical level. However, the objective of the approach which I adopt is to indicate how such threats to the physical body are also layered with connotations. Such meanings become a part of what the 'reality' of the risk is. Once AIDS has been packed with connotations of deviance, for example, the term AIDS comes to stand for 'illness of the deviant'. The simple term AIDS immediately suggests the very antithesis of what is owing to the good, responsible citizen.

Perhaps a greater balance should be struck between material, emotional and social constructionist perspectives in understanding responses to disasters. Recent works on the 'material-discursive' elements of health and illness (e.g Ussher, 1997; Yardley, 1997) and on material-social constructionist angles on emotion (Harré and Parrot, 1996) will ultimately take us further along this road, facilitating an answer to my question concerning the extent to which the material level plays a role in representations of crises.

Concluding remarks

This chapter explored the representations which surround 'the other' in an enduring sense in societies and examined how the negative aspersions cast out onto this entity is magnified at times of imminent mass risk. It provided an overview of the literature on crises ranging from wars to environmental and industrial disasters, and evaluated, in a detailed fashion, social scientific work on reactions to epidemics. It drew together commentaries on responses to potential disasters from a range of disciplines: psychology, cultural theory, history and anthropology. The chapter demonstrated that the 'not me – others' response is common, when people are initially faced with the possibility of being affected by a danger. An explanatory framework for the response to crises, which is developed later in the book, must incorporate both the 'not me' and the 'others are to blame' aspects. To flesh out some of the dynamics of the response to potential danger, in chapter 3 I provide a detailed empirical exploration of a set of responses to a contemporary epidemic which has had the most powerful presence in the developed and developing world since the early 1980s: HIV/AIDS.

NOTES

1 A highly analogous body of evidence for this motif can be found in feminist writing on women as 'other'.
2 This is Hotze's (1856) summary of Gobineau's work, cited in Young (1995: 104).
3 Hottentots are members of a Southern African group of people.

3   A study of lay people's responses to a risk
HIV/AIDS in Britain and South Africa

To shed light on the complex structure of risk-related thought, in this chapter I examine responses to one mass crisis at a particular point in time. I focus on representations of AIDS in the first decade of its advent. I examine the themes that dominate interview talk on the origin, spread and risk of AIDS in Britain and South Africa. Out-groups and in-groups are sampled in both cultures, and I reflect upon the commonality and differences in their representations. The analysis of interview data is set against a backdrop of a thematic analysis of the concurrent medical scientific and mass-mediated ideas. I interweave the findings with the vast literature on early responses to AIDS.

Responses to AIDS in the early years – a depth study of two cultures

Early lay and medical scientific responses to the potential AIDS pandemic provide a fascinating illustration of the link made between mass risk and 'the other'. The lay representations presented in this chapter were gleaned by way of semi-structured interviews with sixty Britons and South Africans. The sample was chosen in accordance with a matched set of criteria to ensure comparability across cultures and groups. A basic criterion for selection was that respondents were urban, young adults with a high level of education. Half of the respondents were British and half South African. They were drawn from three major urban centres in the two countries: London, Johannesburg and Soweto. The average age in the sample was 23 in each country. The majority of the respondents had successfully completed secondary school, with two-thirds, in both countries, being college or university educated. In each of the two countries the sample was composed of white heterosexuals (half were male), black heterosexuals (half were male) and gay men (white and black; a number were HIV positive).

The interviews took place in the early 1990s. In South Africa, they were conducted just before Apartheid was dismantled. The interviews were designed to elicit the respondent's own ideas concerning the origin and spread of AIDS. The questions posed were open. They were as non-directive as possible given the objective of eliciting data which allowed for systematic comparison between interviews. The primary focus was on the following topics: where HIV/AIDS originated, how HIV/AIDS spreads, which group/s are worst affected by AIDS in the respondent's own country and the respondent's personal sense of risk in relation to HIV/AIDS. Each transcribed interview was coded using a computerised system which provided both a qualitative and a quantitative database.[1] The program was employed to generate details of the themes and processes evident in the interviews of individuals, subgroups and the total sample.

Since the ideas advocated by individuals are developed within the context of mass mediated messages, these were also considered. A proliferation of systematic media and health policy analyses examines the prominent features of the social context in which lay thinking was formed in the first decade of AIDS. In addition to drawing upon these studies, I utilise my own systematic analysis of the ideas which circulated in the social context to which lay thinkers had been exposed, at the time of being interviewed. This includes scientific representations, which were ascertained from a thematic analysis of the high-impact medical journals, and an analysis of the public health campaigns on AIDS which had been transmitted in the two cultures.

Cross-cultural, inter-group research is an ideal way of revealing the extent to which ideas are shared or constructed differently within different societies and groups. It is driven by a comparative methodology: sampling is based upon the researcher's suppositions concerning where differences and similarities may lie within a sample. Even with modest samples, it has the capacity to reveal the dynamics of responses to a social phenomenon such as AIDS. The particular advantage of the interview data is that they allow the researcher to explore, in depth, how individuals construct the crisis in their own terms, and then to examine the degree to which in-group and out-group members' ideas resonate with each other. The aim is to allow the dynamics of what underpins such responses to become evident. Since much knowledge about risks originates in the sciences, and gets relayed to lay people via the mass media, medical scientific and mass-mediated ideas about AIDS must also be scrutinised if one is to understand the forces that interact with lay thinking. The distinctive patterns that emerge from studies such as my own can be set against findings from studies which utilise representative samples in order to illustrate the extent to which the findings are generalisable or merely illuminate a more circumscribed aspect of risk-related thought.

Lay thinking: origin, spread and risk of AIDS

Representing the origin of AIDS in terms of a foreign continent

When asked where AIDS originated, most respondents in my study linked it with a continent with which they did not identify. Over three-quarters of the white respondents, in both the British and South African samples, stated that AIDS originated in Africa, while an even greater proportion of black respondents, in both samples, declared that it originated in the West. Of course, the way in which this finding is presented rests upon the assumption that the white people in the sample (be they British or South African) do not identify with Africa, and, similarly, that the black people do not identify with the West. With few exceptions, the interviews are shot through with evidence of this style of identification. The extracts that are presented in this chapter provide an indication of this tendency.

The overriding belief that AIDS must have come from another nation, within my samples, is in keeping with Sabatier's (1988) findings in relation to many cultural responses to AIDS, as well as with evidence from past epidemics (see chapter 2). There are a plethora of studies conducted on representative samples which show that the inhabitants of countries feel that their country will not be affected by AIDS. For example, the vast majority of Agrafiotis' (1990) representative sample of the Athenian population regarded AIDS as a menace to Europe but not to Greece. This is certainly not just a Western tendency. People of African origin in my sample are as likely to link AIDS with their 'other' as the Westerners are. This tendency can also be found in historical, non-Western texts on epidemics, although such documents are less abundant than Western writings.

Representing the spread of AIDS in terms of out-groups

In response to the question concerning how HIV/AIDS spread, one-third of both the British and the South African samples answered by distancing their in-group from AIDS, as demonstrated in excerpts from both countries.[2] Beneath each extract I provide details concerning the identity of the respondent:

It is like word association, isn't it. I think about AIDS I think of drug use, I think of decadent stars [celebrities], I think of homosexuals. I very rarely think of heterosexuals when I think about it . . . when I think about it . . . usually it belongs more to people in the white community . . . It is just the way I've been trained I suppose. Because they tend to do more, I don't know. Their sexuality seems more like perverse. (British black heterosexual male)

In South Africa, we do have immorality but we do have people who stick to their principles: the blacks. (South African black heterosexual male)

Interestingly, these extracts demonstrate that a question about the spread of HIV evokes a blatant denial of the link between these men's in-groups and the spread of HIV. A moralistic judgement concerning 'the other' is also summoned to the respondents' minds by the question: 'perverse' and 'immoral' people are linked to the spread of AIDS. In relation to direct questions concerning their personal risk, over two-thirds of the total sample (excluding those with HIV/AIDS), state that their own chances of contracting HIV are below average.[3] Differences between the gay and heterosexual, white and black, male and female groups are not significant. Furthermore, the Britons and South Africans are equally likely to represent their own vulnerability to HIV as below average. This is compatible with a number of studies (detailed in chapter 4) in which groups materially more at risk of contracting HIV do not show a greater sense of vulnerability to it, when compared with groups materially less at risk. This is termed the 'optimistic bias' in relation to health and safety risks, in the cognitive literature. It can also be construed as denial of vulnerability to danger.

Representing the spread of AIDS in terms of alien practices

In addition to being linked to foreign continents and to out-groups, AIDS is associated with various 'perverse' or 'deviant' practices. Over two-thirds of both the British and South African samples mention at least one of the following five factors in association with the origin and spread of HIV: *aberrant sexuality* (including bestiality and promiscuity); *tribal rituals* (including cannibalism and incest); *'Third World' conditions* (including a lack of Western medicine and overcrowded living conditions); *unhygienic practices*; and the *practices of uneducated people*. One-half of this group combine at least two of the five factors, arriving at a heady combination which I term the 'sin cocktail'. The sin cocktail involves the confounding of two or more 'aberrant' practices, generalising the extent to which they are practised, and linking them to specific groups. The term implies an analogy between the production of potent alcoholic drinks via mixing a range of substances, and the mixing together of different 'sinful' practices, when talking about the origin and spread of AIDS. The end product is more than just a sum of its parts. The following extracts from the interviews are illustrative of the sin cocktail. They are responses to the question 'where did HIV/AIDS originate?' In many instances the question 'how does HIV/AIDS spread?' was answered spontaneously by respondents, as an extension of the answer to the origin question:

Monkeys in Africa. I think that was what I heard and that was passed through God-knows-what to get through [to Britain]. I've heard some extreme stories about how it reached our shore [much laughter]. Which I care not to utter . . . It was just meant to be bestiality, I suppose . . . I could probably imagine it would be something like in their tribe in Africa would probably be more prone to that sort of thing . . . If a man caught it and he had sex with his wife and someone came along, I don't know how these tribes work so I don't know the moral judgement you place on them. Someone could come along and pay some money and have sex with his wife and then he could take it back to his country and give it to his wife. (British white heterosexual male)

The respondent tells a story in which AIDS originates in a monkey on a foreign continent, and reaches the British shore by way of animal–human sexual contact as well as a Western man's engagement in the tribal ritual of wife-lending. The symbolisation of AIDS in practices which take place on a foreign continent is not a mechanism used by Westerners alone, as the following account from a black South African's interview demonstrates:

As I heard it started in England . . . It started between a monkey and a person, after a person intercoursing with a monkey . . . after the person is intercoursing with the monkey he never washed and he went to his partner. Then they intercoursed. Then the partner couldn't hold herself, went and intercoursed with someone else and that is how it spread. He never washed before going to soccer and so AIDS was transmitted to people . . . because in soccer they sweat. Then after getting that sweat he touch me with it and then I've got AIDS. (South African black heterosexual male)

The first of the two extracts locates the origin and spread of HIV/AIDS with 'the other' in relation to the respondent's identity as a Western, white male. The thought processes and contents are remarkably similar in the second extract, though this respondent links the origin and spread of HIV/AIDS to 'the other' of his black, heterosexual identity. The accounts presented are typical of the range of issues which arise in the broader data set. They illustrate a remarkable symmetry: both white and black people imagine 'the other' to be aberrant in terms of sexual rituals, and it is assumed that this spreads, and often even causes, AIDS. Many lay thinkers appear to create a boundary between a self unlinked to any aspects of the illness and an 'other' whose practices lie outside of the boundaries of acceptability in their own societies. I have shown that this 'other' takes on three different forms: people link AIDS with foreign nations, with out-groups and with deviant behaviours. It must be stressed that not everyone in the sample follows this pattern of thought:

a small minority link AIDS with entities closer to themselves and this important issue is developed later in the chapter. I turn to examining medical scientific thinking with regard to HIV/AIDS.

Medical scientific thinking on the origin and spread of AIDS

The lay thinking appears fantastical, a mythical level which stands in opposition to objective, 'scientific facts'. This idea is symbolised in health campaigns which present the prevailing lay 'myths' concerning a particular health issue, alongside the scientific 'truths'. Such campaigns leave their audience in no doubt as to which of the two ways of thinking is the more desirable. Their very aim is to bring all thinking in line with the scientific 'facts'. Yet it is instructive to investigate the unfolding world of 'scientific facts', of 'material realities', at the time that the 'lay myths', illustrated above, were developing. An investigation of the medical scientific ideas which existed in the early stage of the discovery of the AIDS pandemic reveals that the link between foreigners, out-groups, aberrance and disease does not lie exclusively in the psyches of lay individuals. A parallel set of ideas can be found in the medical and media representations of AIDS.

From the very moment that scientists recognised the illness in a small number of people, they linked it to an out-group. The earliest account of what was later termed AIDS (in the US journal *Morbidity and Mortality Weekly*, 5 June 1981) referred to the set of symptoms which had been observed as Gay Related Immune Deficiency (GRID) because the symptom-holders were all gay. American medics initially perceived the newly discovered illness in terms of its relationship to gay identity. Until late in 1983, when AIDS was found to be caused by a virus, the fact that AIDS had principally affected homosexual men prompted medical scientists in search of a cause to look for distinctive features related to homosexual male practice (Wellings, 1988). In 1982 an article in the *Lancet*, for example, postulated that the drug Butyl Nitrite ('poppers'), widely used in the American homosexual community, might impair the body's immune system (Geodert *et al.*, 1982). A further article in the *Lancet* (Lacey and Waugh, 1983) posited that homosexual coitus causes immuno-suppression. When the viral component of AIDS was discovered, talk of practices which led to immune overload temporarily faded from the medical literature. However, the link between the 'homosexual lifestyle' and AIDS lingered in the media and in lay chatter. This had profound effects on the course of the lay representations of AIDS. Herzlich (1973) demonstrates that lay people confound the origin, cause and spread of illness. When a link is made between lifestyle and illness, lay people often imagine that the lifestyle *causes* the illness. The argument that the gay way of life facilitates the attack, by viruses, on the immune system, slid easily into lay representations that the gay lifestyle generates the viruses themselves. Scientific ideas allowed for homosexuality and promiscuity to be established, not merely as facilitators of the spread, but as potential causes, of AIDS: In a representative sample of adults residing in the United States, Herek and Capitano (1993) found that almost half thought that homosexual sex could *cause* AIDS. AIDS could be transmitted between two HIV-negative men who failed to use a condom during sex.

Beyond making the link between AIDS, gay men and their sexual and drug-taking practices, medics associated AIDS with additional foreign peoples, out-groups and deviant practices. The link between AIDS, Haitians, and voodoo practices entered prestigious North American medical journals in the early 1980s, and was conveyed to lay thinkers by the mass media. Farmer (1992) investigated the line of medical thinking which associated AIDS with voodoo practices and concluded: 'North American scientists repeatedly speculated that AIDS might be transmitted between Haitians by voodoo rites, the ingestion of sacrificial animal blood, the eating of cats, ritualized homosexuality and so on – a rich panoply of exotica' (Farmer, 1992: 224). The 'sin cocktail' which I discovered in lay people's accounts of the origin and spread of AIDS is surprisingly similar to this 'panoply of exotica', evident in the medical scientists' understanding of AIDS.

The Haitian-voodoo and homosexual-anal sex-poppers links to AIDS do not complete the picture. The link between AIDS and 'otherness' also exuded from medical reports which claimed a link between Africa, Green monkeys and AIDS: the Green monkey theory became popularised in 1985 when two Harvard professors isolated an HIV-like virus from wild Green monkeys. Many newspapers published stories related to these findings in 1985 (Vass, 1986), linking the Green monkey theory to Africa. Sections of the medical world felt that this link had been firmly established. A haematologist from an eminent Cambridge department wrote, in *Nature* magazine: 'There is now little doubt human AIDS began in Africa. Not only is the disease widely spread in central Africa, but only in Africa are the monkey species naturally infected . . . Although the first such virus was isolated from the macaque, that animal was probably infected in captivity with . . . the African sooty mangabey monkey' (Karpas, 1990:578). Karpas (1990) suggests that the transfer of an HIV-like virus from monkey to human may be related to the sexual habits of the people of the large

African lakes. These people are injected with monkey blood to induce them to intense sexual activity.

The status of the African origin as 'fact', in contemporary social representations of AIDS, is a testimony to the extent to which medical writing concerning AIDS has lived on in the collective imagination.[4] The Green Monkey Theory is one among a number of accounts of the origin. The African Green monkey is not unanimously assumed to harbour a precursor to HIV that crossed the species barrier, in the scientific literature. Hypotheses concerning a laboratory origin, for example, appear in the mainstream scientific literature (Chirimuuta and Chirimuuta, 1989). In addition, whereas there were no allusions to Africa, Africans or travel abroad in the earliest account of AIDS (*Morbidity and Mortality Weekly*, 5 June 1981), the earliest report of AIDS from the perspective of an African medical journal (*East African Medical Journal*, September 1984) was of a Ugandan journalist who had been based in West Germany, London and Nairobi over the years preceding the report (Chirimuuta & Chirimuuta, 1989). This example indicates that certain scientific representations carry greater weight than others, and come to dominate lay thinking. Though one finds evidence of linking AIDS with 'the other' in early Western and non-Western medical journals alike, the Western version has gained a more wide-spread influence the world over.

One repercussion of dominant ideas: spoiled identity in certain groups

Both scientists' and lay thinkers' early responses to AIDS placed its origin with a foreign continent and its spread outside of the in-group, in deviant practices. This limited its potential for personal repercussions. This is part of the 'identity work' which people do: people gain a positive sense of identity through comparison with negatively valued groups. Yet the notion that all groups in a society dissociate their identities from AIDS overlooks the issue of power. Distancing the identity of the in-group and the self via one's representations is inter-linked with the status of the representor in his or her society. Certain identities are constantly attacked in the wider context in which respondents find themselves: gay men's identity had been under threat in an ongoing way in both cultures which I explore, and this censure was heightened when they were linked to the cause of AIDS. Members of stigmatised groups undergo 'identity ambivalence' since they are embedded in the wider norms of the society, norms which view their group as deviant. Yet identification with fellow stigmatised group members binds them to an identity which is seen as offensive and repellent in the broader society. They become ashamed of this identity and thereby gain a 'spoiled identity' (Goffman, 1963). Members of marginalised groups often gain a spoiled identity by internalising the negative aspersions cast out by dominant representations in the society. The interplay between marginalised and dominant ideas is rather complex. By attending to it I hope to demonstrate the value of exploring the accounts given by different group members concerning mass risks.

British gay men have challenged the link that scientists, the mass media and then lay representations have made between their group and AIDS. Voices from the gay movement in Britain formed, maintained and changed the early representations of AIDS through their interaction with the mainstream, historically perpetuated viewpoint (Markova and Wilkie, 1987). The ability to impact upon dominant representations requires that out-groups have a certain amount of power. In the 1970s many British gay people organised themselves into various gay rights movements, created a gay press and were instrumental in abolishing repressive sexual legislation. The Terence Higgins Trust (THT), formed by gay people in 1983 in Britain, had the explicit aim of influencing national policy on AIDS. It instigated the fight against the spread of HIV, disseminating information and setting up help-lines prior to government initiatives. The expansion of the 'gay pride' movement with the advent of AIDS was both a response to the threat of spoiled identity and an attempt to diminish it. At least two factors account for the lack of gay group power in South Africa, in relation to the empowered British gay group, in the first decade of the crisis. South African gay identity contained the fragmentary, non-unified nature of the Apartheid-embedded parent culture (Isaacs and McKendrick, 1992). Splits along racial lines, for example, contributed to its fragmentation. This left the movement far less powerful, both in numbers and in its capacity to impose its voice on widespread representations of AIDS. In addition, in keeping with this undemocratic nature of the society, no attempt was made to give marginalised groups a voice in early AIDS policy formation. By way of contrast, the THT was not only recognised as a legitimate mouthpiece and forger of gay safer sexual practices in Britain, but was also funded by the government to make heterosexually targeted AIDS campaigns in 1990. A marginalised group's voice was being allowed to impact upon the AIDS-related thoughts of the 'general public'.

I have shown that the origin and spread of AIDS tends to be linked with foreign continents, and a specific set of out-groups, by all groups. Yet those groups who are constantly held responsible for AIDS, in the dominant representations of each of the two societies which I studied, view themselves (and their in-group) as both affected by and responsible for AIDS. Risk is often denied when the question is asked directly. Yet internalisation of the link between the self and the risk seeps into other areas of the interview. All groups have their own repertoire of perverse out-groups with whom AIDS may be associated. Yet gay men, in particular, also show signs of internalising the dominant representation concerning themselves, viewing themselves as 'disgusting', responsible for, and deserving of, AIDS. Despite the strength of the 'gay pride' movement, the majority of the gay men in Britain show signs of these feelings. This is vividly illustrated in many extracts:

I am gay myself, but gay people are so damned disgusting. Um, you've got, I mean, let's not beat about the bush here . . . the element is so strong whereby now we are living in an age whereby a man will approach a man in broad daylight . . . there's a lot of deviant behaviour going on and that's, I'm not saying it's wrong, but I, it's certainly deviant, you know. (British black gay male)

On some unconscious level the sort of idea of AIDS being punishment for gay people might have permeated my brain. (British white gay male)

I had a test and I was negative, thank God, and I put it down to, it's not that God was fair, he just didn't want me basically, just didn't want to know. He like, you know, 'there's no room for this one here'. (British black gay male)

Signs of having internalised the society's association between their groups and AIDS were evident in almost half of the gay men in the total sample, and in a similar proportion of black, heterosexual South Africans. The internalisation of the internationally pervasive link between AIDS and Africans, as well as the endorsement of this link in South Africa, may go some way to explaining this.[5] One South African, black heterosexual respondent, frightened that he may have AIDS, used blackness to symbolise the foreboding appearance of a person with AIDS. He appeared to be drawing on a vision of a person with Kaposi Sarcoma, the cancer which produces black blotches on the skin:

I think now I have got the AIDS so I said I better stop [sexual activity] . . . I just imagine that his [a person with AIDS] appearance, he is black, I mean he seems to be a dark, dark black, and then starts sometimes to become thin. Others become fat. Then start having these big, big things. I don't know what you call it . . . people are running away from him, the way he looks. Terrible, terrible person. (South African black heterosexual male)

These examples indicate that the explanation espoused by a particular individual is not always consistent with the 'not me – not my group' pattern. This is a key contribution which interview-based work can make to theories of the response to risks. Spoiled identity, the internalisation of stigmatising ideas concerning one's group (Goffman,

1963), manifests strongly in the out-group members who were inter-viewed. Identification with fellow stigmatised group members binds the stigmatised to a deviant identity which is seen as offensive and repellent in the broader society. The stigmatised manifest shame in relation to this identity. It is important to note that while this process was in evidence, it was not evident in all out-group members and even those who showed self-disgust often held contradictory, 'not me – others', ideas simultaneously. The most salient indicator of this was that in relation to a direct question concerning personal risk, most HIV nega-tive gay men saw their chances of contracting HIV as below average.

The accounts of those who had been most closely linked with the AIDS crisis in the wider cultural context bore a further theme, related to the spoiled sense of identity. British gay and black men in the sample, but not South Africans or heterosexual white Britons, were likely to posit conspiracy theories concerning the origin and spread of AIDS. These conspiracy theories must be viewed in light of the worldwide links that were being made between AIDS and Africans.

A consequence of spoiled identity: conspiracy theories

The vast majority of the British black group and half of the British gay groups in my sample threw blame for AIDS back at the dominant group. They imagined that dominant groups had engineered the AIDS pandemic. Conspiracy theories of AIDS have been pervasive among out-groups in many cultural settings (e.g. see Aggleton et al., 1989; Dalton, 1989; Farmer, 1992). Like the mainstream 'not me – others are to blame' theories, they locate responsibility for the threat externally.

In my data, a specific group, Western scientists, provide a focus not only for the black British sample's feelings of disdain, but also for their admiration. Western scientists and technologists are imagined to be cruel, dangerous and omnipotent. By accentuating their power, they also become construed as awe-inspiring. This resonates with the mixed denigration and admiration of 'the other' in Western thinking, which I traced in chapter 2. The 'other' is admired for qualities that one's own group lacks. A widespread line of reasoning in the black Britons' accounts is that the genesis of AIDS is connected to Western experi-mentation. Science and technology interferes, it precipitates an imbal-ance in the natural order. The term 'science' is read as 'tampering' by many of the British respondents who belong to marginalised groups:

The West they are always experimenting, they are always finding out new, they are always coming up with theories – if you do this what happens. They are always experimenting. So to me, along that line, they must experiment with something that can develop into AIDS that created the disease AIDS, because AIDS didn't come out of nowhere. Where was it one, two hundred years ago, people weren't dying, it must have come now. It is not more than fifty, sixty years old. It is a very new disease. It is not like the old diseases. So the only way, so the only way it could have come is for someone to make a mistake along the line and create a disease like that. (British black heterosexual male)

This account links contemporary, Western practices with the conditions that 'create a disease'. The respondent vacillates between the wilful and the mistaken creation of AIDS. Contemporary society is represented as a laboratory. The black Britons, in general, move between regarding the laboratory antics of Westerners as relatively benign, and construing them as overtly malicious:

There's good chance of it being an experiment . . . It could be used as a weapon I suppose, it could be used as a weapon, I don't know. The Americans get up to a lot of things, you know? People think they're the most innocent people but they're not, there's a lot of things that goes on behind shut doors. I reckon they could have sort of formed it as a weapon or just a daily experiment, one of the experiments they do there, in laboratories . . . Yeah, there are the chances that it could have been an experiment of like maybe an animal had this unknown disease or whatever, and they probably took samples of its blood or whatever, could have been a monkey, a chimpanzee, anything you know, and it could have leaked out, it's one of those possibilities, and you know, bit like Chernobyl type of thing. (British black heterosexual male)

A link is forged between nuclear disaster and the origins of AIDS. The message is that scientists cannot be trusted. At best they are dangerously incompetent. At worst they manufacture weapons of mass destruction targeted at out-groups:

I actually think the AIDS virus was sort of invented in a laboratory. I think it was invented years ago probably in the 1960s or something, and so now it's got out. I don't know why they did it, they needed it to control the population or something. I think there's an antidote as well, but they waiting for a right time to release it. (British black heterosexual female)

A further participant augments this idea:

1960s, they [the Americans] had . . . these ideas to forcibly put something in water of Third World countries to stop . . . .against the government's wishes, to stop them from having babies . . . they don't want to be swamped. I mean, America is, I mean Europe is getting together – they're tightening up, aren't they? They're saying how they want to keep immigration people out, immigration out . . . I think we should try to get to the bottom of how it got about, but I just feel about it being manufactured as a population control. (British black heterosexual male)

The invention of HIV for the purpose of population control, which includes control of immigrant populations – keeping the foreign 'other' out – is one manifestation of the malevolent Western practices put forward by the black Britons. Another is the creation and use of HIV as a means of biological warfare:

I think it was a scientific development by the Americans in the Vietnam War. They were trying to make a killer disease to kill all the Vietnamese people and it went wrong, and they was testing it on monkeys, this is what I've been told, they was testing it on monkeys and some like nasty people must have buggered the monkeys and caught it from them. (British black heterosexual male)

In this sin cocktail the man shifts from a notion that Americans act sinfully by creating a 'killer disease' to their bestial practices with the research monkeys. A generalised sense of the malicious 'other' is present, which mirrors the Western notions of bestiality and tribal rituals in 'darkest' Africa.

Interestingly, one of these black British respondents makes a very direct link between the creation of AIDS and the Tuskegee study. This theme manifests more covertly in the other accounts. This is important in that it indicates that historically salient ideas live on in a group's representations and are drawn upon when new threats must be assimilated. The Tuskegee study was a syphilis experiment in Alabama, which lasted from 1932 to 1972. Researchers chose not to treat 600 black men with syphilis so that they could observe the progress of the disease (Brandt, 1978).[6] Respondents suggest that the origin of AIDS may contain similarities:

I reckon America has got a lot to do with it, a lot more to do with it than we think. I've read about it . . . in the 1940s where a group of black GI prisoners of war were contaminated with hepatitis or syphilis or what's the name. They were let back into the community just to see. So they gave it to their wives and their children and it seems they used them like guinea pigs really, they didn't tell them that they had it, you see. Now if something like that could of happened, it doesn't surprise me that something like that could of happened [with AIDS] as well. (British black heterosexual male)

Despite the fact that members of the black British sample were embedded in Western culture, by dint of the fact that they lived in Britain, their responses suggest identification with those who were the targets of American conspiracies, including birth control in underdeveloped countries. When compared with a matched group of white heterosexual Britons talking about AIDS, the black heterosexual Britons are far more likely to associate it with humans having actively tampered with populations by way of technology. The black British sample views AIDS as a deleterious consequence of Western interference with the balance of nature, in a similar fashion to the Ngubane findings concerning Zulu representations of illness (see chapter 2). The black Britons also links the genesis of other disasters – such as Chernobyl and the spread of syphilis and hepatitis – to Western interference. Disdain is shown with regard to such tampering. Yet, simultaneously, there is a fascination implied in depicting the horrors and abuses perpetuated by 'Westerners'. This is the mirror image of the Western 'sin cocktail' and the Western 'panoply of exotica'. Even though these people, strictly speaking, cannot be considered 'non-Westerners', their accounts are interesting in that they mirror the Western accounts of illness in terms of their patterning and their content.

I have indicated that explanations of AIDS which suggest the involvement of a conspiracy must be situated against a historic backdrop in which, on a material level, out-groups *were* used for population control and experimentation. The most salient example of this, which out-group publications have brought to the attention of their readers, is the American Tuskegee Institute's experiment. The Tuskegee experiment is just one of many concerning out-groups, including the eugenics-based experiments on Jews by the Nazis. The media's role in alerting certain groups to these studies is vital since without the widespread dissemination of the Tuskegee findings, black Britons would not have known about it.

It would be surprising if a history of indifference to the well-being of certain communities, or the material infliction of hardship upon them, did not influence community members' explanations of new, seemingly similar disasters. Yet in South Africa neither the black nor the gay groups in my sample advocated conspiracy theories. This may relate to a whole gamut of factors, including the ideological and physical repression of these groups which was still under way in the first decade of the AIDS crisis. It may also be linked to the absence of such theories in the publications to which South Africans were exposed at the time that the interviews took place. Interestingly, such theories appeared in *Drum*, a South African, urban, black-targeted general interest magazine, the year after my interviews were conducted, when Apartheid began its demise. The article explained the conspiracy involved in the Tuskegee study and warned of its parallel to the AIDS crisis.

The mass media's role in shaping thoughts on the origin and spread of AIDS

I have indicated that scientific writing and lay thinking both revealed the 'not me – others' response. Yet the processes in the scientific and lay spheres do not merely run on parallel lines. Science provides the seeds of many lay thoughts regarding risks. There can be no contention that AIDS was initially 'discovered' in the world of medical science. Consequently, lay thinkers must have learned of the syndrome via assimilation of what were originally scientific ideas. Since the majority of lay thinkers do not have direct access to medical journals, they are exposed to such ideas via the interpretations offered by the mass media. Before exploring one aspect of the early media message about AIDS, I need to signal that I am not positing a causal model in which lay thinkers passively absorb scientific ideas. Rather, it can be argued that lay thinkers negotiate the meaning of ideas which are transmitted from the scientific world, in forming their own responses. Yet the range of meanings is constrained by the set of ideas to which they are exposed: whereas, to my knowledge, medics attempting to explain the spread of HIV did not suggest African bestiality as a form of contact between Green monkey and human, this representation of scientific thinking is not very far afield from the ideas that *were* put forward by the scientists. Scientific talk of the simian HIV-like virus approximating the human one and Karpas' sexually based theories lend themselves to this type of representation.

The key mediators between scientific and lay ideas are the mass media. A plethora of studies examines the media's presentation of AIDS. In the early years, a link between AIDS and 'the other' was found in many of the studies. Wellings (1988), for example, indicated that in the first few years of the epidemic, AIDS was 'virtually synonymous with the term "gay plague" in national press reportage in Britain' (1988: 84). In addition, Kitzinger and Miller (1991) found a match between British audience ideas about AIDS and television news items. In both, AIDS was 'blamed on African sexuality which is presented as primitive and perverse and associated with homosexuality and bestiality' (Kitzinger and Miller, 1991: 12).

A further element of the mass media which shaped (and was shaped by) lay ideas was the early government-funded campaign transmitted to allay the spread of AIDS. Government public health campaigns are particularly important in terms of elucidating the link between scientific and lay representations of risks for a number of reasons. Campaigns represent a central, official position which crystallises what has been deemed a desirable message in the public health policy realm. Such campaigns react to existing ideas in the society and also set the terms of future debates. The early AIDS campaigns in the two cultures which I studied had a major and long-lasting impact. Both had a very wide audience reception: approximately 82 per cent of British adults (Department of Health and Social Security and the Welsh Office, 1987) and 80 per cent of South Africans (McCann Group, 1988) saw an aspect of the early campaign. Furthermore, the first wave of the British AIDS campaign was still most salient in people's minds after a number of subsequent waves of the campaign (Wellings, 1988). The earliest, wide-spread images of a phenomenon have a great and lasting impact. This may well be linked to a primacy effect. I shall present key themes that emerged from the early campaigns in the two countries.

Certain aspects of the early government campaigns reflected (and shaped) the lay and scientific tendency to cast AIDS out onto 'the other'. In particular, in the early depiction of AIDS, ideas concerning 'leakage' (Watney, 1987) from infected out-groups to a wider public were conveyed. Newspaper, television and cinema advertisements in the 1986–87 British 'Don't die of ignorance' campaign claimed: 'At the moment the infection is mainly confined to relatively small groups of people in this country. But the virus is spreading'. The early South African campaigns carried a similar message. Although black and white South Africans were targeted by separate campaigns, both contained a logo that depicted a map of Africa in which the north and south were white while central Africa was red. This symbolises the AIDS-ridden nature of central Africa. One implication was that South Africa, pre-sently in a fortunate position, may become red or polluted with HIV. This sense of the march of AIDS through Africa was conveyed in accompanying television advertisements in which the 'red' HIV threat was shown to be gaining an increasing grip on Africa. The message was that there was still a chance to keep South Africa relatively AIDS-free, with monogamy suggested as the key tool, since it was 'the other' who was presently affected.

The content of such campaigns was interlinked with a fear-evoking style, in both cultures. Fear-evocation tactics were present in the words, which threatened contagion, as well as in the imagery of the campaigns: tombstone and iceberg imagery characterised the first major British campaign. In the earliest South African television cam-paign a differential threat was posed to black as opposed to white people, yet some level of danger was present in both campaigns. The black-targeted campaign depicted a coffin and funeral scene along with the slogan 'The new killer disease is here'. The white-targeted cam-paign presented a graffiti-ridden wall and stated that 'the writing could be on the wall' if safety measures were not adopted. AIDS was represented as being only temporarily confined to 'risk groups': it threatened to invade the entire community. It was against the backdrop of these fear-evoking representations, with their widespread audience reception that lay people began to formulate their ideas concerning AIDS and to assess their own vulnerability to it.

Interestingly, the large-scale survey, conducted for the Department of Health and Social Security (DHSS) comparing the attitudes of the

British public before, and then a year into, the 'don't die of ignorance' campaign, found an 'increase in feelings that AIDS sufferers "only have themselves to blame"' (DHSS, 1987: 19). Despite increases in awareness and knowledge linked to HIV and AIDS, self-reported behaviour had not changed and blame had increased.

The campaigns were received alongside news, feature and documentary items which contained links between Africa, monkeys and AIDS, and gay promiscuity and AIDS, in both countries. The representations which had been present at the point of assimilation of the new phenomenon lingered in the lay accounts offered to me. They may have contributed to an ongoing denial of vulnerability to AIDS in both Britain and South Africa. Not only was AIDS linked to 'the other' explicitly, but also in being presented as an extremely scary phenomenon which had the potential to leak into the entire population, it elicited defensive, protective reactions. Its connection to the self was denied and AIDS was externalised.

Concluding remarks

My study showed that the fundamental dynamic, when faced with the AIDS risk in the first decade of its advent, was to form representations which distanced the self and in-group from it. Having established the widespread existence of the 'not me – others' phenomenon in talk about AIDS in a sample of lay thinkers in two cultures, which complements findings concerning other epidemics and other risks, I am in a position to explore why this occurs. The black/white divide, within both the British and the South African samples, concerning the content of representations of the origin and spread of AIDS, raises a strong possibility that an identity protective process is at work. The content of each group's representations contains diseased others and healthy selves. This content is also evident in the various mass mediated representations, and in Western scientists' proclivity to link the origin of the spread of HIV/AIDS with non-Western nations and with out-groups, and the mirroring of this pattern in non-Western scientists' accounts.

The black Britons' accounts of the origin and spread of AIDS are highly relevant to a theory of the response to risks. They corroborate the notion of contemporary failure of trust in the experts, put forward in the 'risk society' hypothesis (Beck, 1986/1992; see also chapter 1). In particular, constant experimentation with new technologies, for which no-one is accountable, creates high levels of anxiety. Raised anxiety may well account for the need to re-project blame for AIDS among a group who have themselves been the target of the projections levelled by dominant groups. Conspiracy theories are a way of distancing the in-group from the source of AIDS. They are the rhetorical defence of the black Britons. I have stated that people's representations reveal identity work which limits the repercussions of the danger for themselves. However, while both in-groups and out-groups place blame for the origin and spread of risk with other parties, simultaneously, they may be all too aware of how the actions of 'others' expose them to potential danger.

A crucial feature of empirical work on risk is that it demonstrates that any overriding claims concerning 'public' responses to risks must be tempered. The distinctions between how different groups explain risks are sometimes difficult to make in sociological, historical and cultural studies of crises. While my data indicate that different groups talk about the crisis differently, in terms of the underlying 'not me – others' process, the similarities are stark.

In order to capture the complexity of the range of factors which need to be considered in the response to risk, a close look at one area of threat has been chosen. The advantage of the interview-based approach is that it indicates that explanations of AIDS given by various group members centre on identity negotiation. The 'we' that lives within the 'I' becomes all too apparent when people talk about this crisis. The black Britons who worry and wonder whether AIDS is a conspiracy like that which affected black people in the United States, make this all too apparent. Similarly, spoiled identity indicates that dominant ideas can enter the psyche and make for subjective feelings of self-disgust. The ability to generalise from responses to AIDS to other areas of threat cannot be assumed. In chapter 4 I look into the empirical work on feelings of invulnerability to a broad range of health and safety risks.

NOTES

1 Textbase Alpha was used.
2 The excerpts presented are selected on the basis that they reflect themes common to many respondents, and that they illustrate these themes particularly well.
3 Since my concern in this book is with the feelings of vulnerability to risk among those who are not affected, some of the interesting patterns of thought that emerge in the subgroup of gay men who had HIV/AIDS at the time when the interviews were conducted have not been conveyed. These are laid out most fully in Joffe (1995) but are also alluded to in Joffe (1996a). In addition, Crossley (1997) talks of patterns of projection of the AIDS threat among

people with HIV. Imagining that others are more at risk of death leaves people with HIV with a sense of their own invulnerability.

4 Fresh evidence concerning cross-species transmission of primate retroviruses to humans reinforces such beliefs (e.g. see volume 397 of *Nature*, 1999). Hunting or husbandry in central Africa are the key practises currently linked with the cross-species transfer. Weiss and Wrangham (1999) state: 'Hunters dismember chimpanzees with primitive butchery, and so expose themselves to the risk of zoonotically transmitted disease' (p. 385). The material basis of such findings is not the focus here (see chapter 2). Rather, where medical scientists look for 'facts' and *how* they look, are under scrutiny.

5 I conducted interviews with AIDS policy-makers who belonged to the National AIDS Advisory Group (NAAG) of South Africa in 1989. More than one member stated that it was the black community, as opposed to the white, who would become the major source of AIDS in the country. Talk of the link between homosexuality and AIDS was not pervasive, though there was considerable allusion to how the South African pattern was like the Western pattern (i.e. one in which the majority of the people with AIDS were gay men). This mapped onto the AIDS statistics of the day since 75 per cent of the people with AIDS in South Africa were white men who had contracted HIV through gay sex. The non-Western distribution of AIDS cases supplanted this pattern, in the 1990s.

6 The experiment was viable because it was conducted under the auspices of a respected body: the US government. The cohort was chosen on the basis that its members already had syphilis. Yet when penicillin became widely available in the 1950s and was deemed effective for the treatment of syphilis, the men were not given the drug. Black Alabamans participated in the experiment under the assumption that they were being given treatment, yet the treatments were all placebos. The experimenters went even further. They sought to ensure that the subjects did not receive treatment from other sources, over the forty-year period in which the study took place.

4   Evaluating two social psychological models of the response to risks

The concept of risk perception emerged from work carried out in the 1950s by health service psychologists in the United States. They were interested in how people think about the health and safety risks they face. Their goal was to forge predictive models concerning health-related behaviour. These models have the perceived risk of becoming ill or perceived vulnerability to illness as a central feature. Research on this variable gained considerable impetus in the 1980s when Weinstein and his colleagues discovered that the majority of people are 'unrealistically optimistic' in relation to a large range of health and safety risks. While early disaster work was concerned with the role of unconscious defensiveness in responses to mass threats, by the 1980s the focus on the unconscious had been cognitivised, and denial had been conceptualised as 'optimistic bias' (OB). This chapter focuses on research conducted within the cognitive psychological rubric, including both OB and the older field of attribution theory. This work is evaluated, with an eye to discerning the assumptions it makes.

Theorising the response to crisis in mainstream social psychology

Optimistic bias: comparative risk judgements and the 'not me' phenomenon

The OB framework demonstrates that humans tend to respond self-protectively when asked to assess their risk of being affected by a potential hazard. They imagine, unrealistically, that the future holds few adverse events (Taylor, 1989) and expect such events to strike others, rather than themselves (Weinstein, 1982). Weinstein's (1987) influential work on OB, in particular, confirms the robust and widespread nature of this tendency in terms of a range of health and safety risks. This includes: drug addiction, alcohol problems, attempting suicide, asthma, food poisoning, nervous breakdown, pneumonia, lung cancer, skin cancer, senility, tooth decay, insomnia, ulcers, becoming a victim of a mugging and contracting diabetes, among many other health and safety risks. The early focus was on more commonplace risks than the mass risks which I have highlighted, but more recent studies have also found the OB effect in relation to mass risks such as that of radiation and AIDS.

Risk-related optimism appears to be a widespread phenomenon, which is not associated with age, gender, education or occupation. Taylor and Brown (1994) go as far as to assert that, typically, above 95 per cent of the population exhibit unrealistic risk-related optimism. Optimism is unrelated to whether a risk is perceived as minor or major, or to whether the respondent is at high or at low risk in material terms. The key factor that does affect 'unrealistic' optimism is the perceived preventability of the risk: people are more unrealistic about the risks inherent in hazards which are perceived as preventable, than those that are not.

Unrealistic optimism is defined in the optimistic bias literature as the underestimation of the likelihood or probability of experiencing negative events (Weinstein and Klein, 1996) expressed in the consistent tendency to assert that one's own chances of being affected by a risk are lower than the chances of one's peers (Weinstein, 1987). It is linked with the belief that one is more likely to experience pleasant events and less likely to experience negative events than one's peers (Myers and Brewin, 1996). The key point underlying this concept is that it is impossible for most people to be better off than the *average person*, to whom they are asked to compare themselves. Since it is statistically impossible for most members of a population to be better off than 'the average person', many members must be demonstrating a biased perception.

Denial of susceptibility to risks is not generally related to actual practice: people are equally likely to be unrealistically optimistic, whatever their chances of coming into contact with a risk. Weinstein (1987) was careful to explore the material basis of a person's risks when judging whether someone is optimistically biased or not: 'If an individual claims that his or her susceptibility to a particular hazard is less than average, we cannot conclude that this is an example of unrealistic optimism. Such a claim may be perfectly correct' (Weinstein, 1987: 489). In order to ascertain whether people's evaluations are correct or not, he looked at the correlation between people's comparative risk judgements and their actual risk-taking behaviours. In general, there is no link between the perception of risk and the material risk (e.g. see Hansen, *et al.*, 1990). There are, however, some more equivocal findings regarding this aspect. Certain studies contradict this robust finding. Feldman *et al.* (1997)

studied a sample of Zambian adolescents. The vast majority saw AIDS as a serious threat to their local community and to themselves and most (76 per cent) knew someone with, or who had died of, AIDS. However, over half (55 per cent) said that their chances of getting AIDS were nil or very small. One inference from these findings is that they support the notion of optimistic bias at a group level and that what members of the sample see in the abstract, they do not apply to the concrete circumstance of themselves contracting HIV. However, at an individual level, safe practices correlate with low perceptions of risk. Those who are less at risk, in terms of reported behaviour, are more likely to feel invulnerable, in this study. Realism rather than optimism prevails.

Despite this aberration, from Weinstein's perspective, the majority of the studies found that a person's level of OB differs according to a number of variables, unrelated to the 'real' likelihood of being affected by the adverse event. An interesting social variable is *who* people are cued to compare themselves to, when thinking about their chances of being faced by a risk. If they are asked to compare themselves to an 'average' or 'typical' other, comparative optimism occurs. Yet if comparisons are requested to a closest friend, siblings or same sex-parent, no optimism manifests (Perloff and Fetzer, 1986). People even show OB *on behalf of* people who are close to them: in relation to a close friend, but not for an acquaintance (Regan *et al.*, 1995; Otten and van der Pligt, 1996). Perhaps people lend their own perspective on themselves, when judging those who are experienced to be a part of the extended self. Even though researchers working in this field tend not to dwell on it, the findings concerning protection of those people who are experienced as close to the self indicate that factors beyond individual protection are at work. People are optimistically biased on behalf of those to whom they are close, and view their risks to be similar to this in-group. Findings from the other social sciences (see chapter 2) demonstrate that a positive sense of group, and therefore self, identity is augmented by representing other groups as more vulnerable to negative forces, such as disasters and illnesses.

A fundamental determinant of OB is the perception that becoming affected by the risk is preventable by individual action.[1] The issues of preventability and control have received considerable attention in this literature and have been a locus of study from the earliest psychological works on judging crises. Harris and Middleton (1994) go as far as to state that OB is, in a sense, a tendency to perceive events to be more under personal control than they actually are. People are unrealistically optimistic about negative events that are perceived to be under their control (Harris, 1996) and tend to see themselves as having control over events, even those heavily determined by chance (see Taylor and Armor, 1996).[2]

There is debate concerning whether control is more highly valued in the West than outside of it. Based upon a comparison of a North American and a Japanese sample, Kleinhesselink and Rosa (1991) posit that Westerners tend to see risks in a more controllable light than non-Westerners do. This certainly corroborates Crawford's (1994) theory that religious and secular factors have led Western cultures to place considerable value on self-control (see chapter 2). The smattering of studies that make a comparison between Western and non-Western OB shows that it exists beyond the West, but often to a smaller degree. Heine and Lehman (1995) show that Canadians have significantly greater optimistic bias compared to Japanese people on all future negative events included in their study. However, in a study of Poles, Belgians and Moroccans, Peeters et al. (1997) found that samples from all three cultures manifested similar amounts of OB. The level of optimism differed according to the potential problem being evaluated, rather than according to the culture of the respondent. OB was also evident in a sample of Singaporean students, the vast majority of whom had Chinese backgrounds (Lek and Bishop, 1995).

If OB is closely linked with an exaggerated sense of self-control, then this sense must be present outside of Western cultures. In their review of the positive illusions literature, Taylor and Armor (1996) propose that positive illusions exist in most cultures but that the specific form which they take is culturally specific. Principally, while the *individual's* sense of control in relation to risks is emphasised in Western cultures, in societies where interdependence is stressed, there is an emphasis on the control that *groups* or *cultures* have, to forestal potentially negative events.

A number of objections to the proposed ubiquity of the OB phenomenon have come from the individual differences camp. They claim that the group criterion used in much of the OB literature, regarding the average comparative risk across a sample, does not tell the researcher exactly who manifests these biased judgements. A few extremely positive people may skew the distribution (Myers and Brewin, 1996). From this vantage point, most people are neither optimistic nor pessimistic, but realistic. The extremely optimistic minority skews the overall picture. The findings from the Zambian study (cited on pp. 57–58), corroborate this. In a similar vein Gladis et al. (1992) demonstrate that those in their sample who perceived themselves to be at higher risk were those whose behaviour was, in fact, riskier. For these authors, many people are realistic about their risks but a small group, termed 'repressers' are dispositionally prone to dealing with threatening stimuli via avoidance.

Denial, motivated by fear, exists in just a quarter of their sample and is linked to unrealistic perceptions of risk. There is a growing body of work on those who are extremely optimistic or in a state of perpetual denial. However, at the other end of the spectrum, there may well be excessively pessimistic individuals who worry excessively about each and every potential danger. Evidence concerning their impact upon the distribution of comparative risk assessments is less conclusive.

Interestingly, even though Taylor and Brown (1994) differ radically from Gladis *et al.* (1992) in terms of the proportion of people who they find hold unrealistic perspectives on their risk, both propose that denial underpins it. I turn now to examining explanations of what underpins OB. Weinstein's work is highly equivocal on this point. It veers towards rejection of the denial hypothesis. Rather than OB revealing a defensive sense of denial in the face of anxiety, Weinstein (1987) claims that he has evidence that OB is caused by cognitive errors. An information processing error, such as the differential availability of information occurs: one's lack of experience with the problem makes it difficult to imagine how it might affect oneself. People may also compare themselves with others who are at particularly high risk, in order to maintain a sense of low personal risk. Alternatively, they overestimate their own skills, skills that would allow them to avoid being affected by the risk. These cognitive tricks allow people to maintain positive self-esteem.

Since the late 1970s a lot of the research on judgements that occur in situations of uncertainty has been driven by the attempt to discover the different biases which affect all stages of human judgement. This has led to the compilation of a large list of heuristics and biases (Budescu and Bruderman, 1995). Within the mainstream risk-perception literature the resistance to making a link between oneself and risk is always framed in terms of cognitive faults rather than in emotional terms: 'OB' rather than 'denial'. The notion of optimistic 'bias' implies that people should be unbiased, but that certain errors enter into their judgements. This implication is even more pronounced in the stream of cognitive research which looks at people's actual, numerical risk estimates and where they falter. My argument is that even if lay people had full access to all of the scientific findings associated with the likelihood of the adverse event affecting them, they would not necessarily react in accordance with scientific logic.

Within these mainstream traditions of psychology, humans are assumed to be rational information processors, who make mistakes in thinking about risk probabilities, due to cognitive illusions. The fact that scientists have problems with accurate risk assessment is obscured by studies of faulty, lay, risk assessment. Precise assessment of the risk posed by global warming, for example, is virtually impossible (Giddens, 1991). Even when scientists are able to accurately assess the likelihood of people being affected by a misfortune in the future, and of the magnitude of the damage, they can offer only averages, prevalence rates for a population or sample. Information about one's own subjective likelihood of being faced by the risk is extremely difficult to assess. The risk of contracting cancer from radiated mushrooms, post-Chernobyl, for example, would involve an intricate formula which accounted for myriad factors ranging from how many one had eaten to the proximity of one's home from the fall-out.

The vision of the human as a faulty information processor is problematic not only because the 'true' risks posed to individuals by dangers are often impossible to calculate. The focus on the human information processing system also has problematic implications for the extent to which emotions feature in our understanding of this human. Inherent in an information processing approach is the view that the human mind is analogous to a machine. By definition, the feeling element of being alive is thereby underplayed. The focus on information processing thereby obscures that which is distinctive about being human.

To a great extent, Weinstein's work is a cognitivisation of an earlier psycho-dynamic strand of thought, in which denial and the projection onto others were posited as key responses to the anxiety evoked by dangers (e.g. see Baker and Chapman, 1962). Weinstein's early work explicitly tested this approach. Though his findings support the hypothesis that people disavow their links to adverse events, he rejects the link to unconscious defensiveness. The foundations of this claim lie in a very specific empirical finding: the negative correlation between respondents' rating of the degree of worry that people feel about a particular hazard, and optimism. Weinstein assumes that respondents should manifest more optimism on the hazards that are perceived as more threatening than on what are perceived as more minor risks, if defensive processes are at work. In fact, the higher the score on one of his measures of threat, the lower the level of optimism (e.g. Weinstein, 1987).

This finding is equivocal within the OB literature and even within Weinstein's own work (see Hoorens, 1994). In their review, Taylor and Armor (1996) argue that human perception reveals evidence of positive illusions in an ongoing sense, and that there is mounting evidence that when a negative event threatens the individual, positive illusions increase. A vivid illustration of this is provided by Taylor et al. (1992) who examined the optimistic beliefs about AIDS in a sample of gay men at risk of HIV infection. The study indicates that the men who know they are HIV positive in the sample are significantly *more* optimistic about not developing AIDS than the men who know they do not have HIV. In line with the notion of unconscious coping mechanisms, for these authors OB is a defensive means of coping with threat.

Taylor and colleagues' findings are corroborated by many studies, though counter-evidence, such as that of the Zambian study, exists. Before delving into a fascinating piece of research which supports both the defensive and cognitive limitation hypotheses, it is useful to reflect upon the method by which data are gleaned in the majority of OB studies. An assumption is made that people have a high level of access to states of concern about the magnitude of risks, and can calibrate them accurately on scales. Yet it may be imprudent to assume that the range of factors which feed the 'not me' response will be found within what the individual can tell the researcher. Motives which have not reached consciousness may influence this response. If one considers the limitations of self-reports (see chapter 7), development of theory concerning implicit processes may be crucial. Underpinning the Weinstein model is an assumption that humans are basically risk averse but unintentionally take risks due to cognitive deficits such as an inefficient handling of information. Perhaps the 'logic' of risk aversion is not a probabilistic one: people may know that smoking leads to lung cancer but they may be smoking to facilitate mental well-being (Graham, 1987), with cancer not at the forefront of their concerns. So the model of the human built into OB may not contain an accurate understanding of how the human mind operates. People may make comparisons between the different risks faced, rather than the locus of comparison being other people's perceived risk, which is imposed by the method of the Weinstein model.

In an interview-based, rather than rating-scale-based study, Sobo (1995) focused on the unsafe sexual understandings and practices of black North American women in the inner cities. The study was conceived within a cognitive OB model, but incorporated a rich array of emotional and cultural factors. It provided a prototype for an enriched use of the OB paradigm. It demonstrated that emotional defence, as well as errors of judgement, motivate OB. The study was set against a statistical backdrop in which the majority of women with HIV and AIDS in the United States are poor, black and live in urban areas. Black North American women, in general, have a higher than average chance of contracting HIV. The heterosexual mode of transmission is most common in this group. The majority of the women who get AIDS are infected by way of condomless sex with long-term partners. The high infectivity rates appear to be related to the practices of the men. Men, but not women, with partners are expected to have extra-conjugal affairs. Weinberg and Williams (1988) report that 76 per cent of black North American men have extra-conjugal affairs. Despite sex with such men constituting a highly risky activity, the majority of Sobo's female sample believe that they are *not* at risk of contracting HIV when they have unsafe sex with their partners.

This belief hinges on two narratives regarding the self which contain opposite narratives regarding others. The self is not at risk because the self's partners are monogamous, and the self is wise enough to choose such partners. However, other women are not sharp enough to spot the unfaithful man: 'all men, except one's own, are bound to "mess around"' (Sobo, 1995: 118). Sobo states that OB underpins this way of explaining the world. Impoverished inner-city women idealise mono-gamy and wish for loyal conjugal partners: 'In some senses then unsafe sex is an *adaptive and defensive practice*. It helps women maintain desired, idealised images of partners, relationships and selves' (Sobo, 1995: 195, my italics). Sobo combines this implicitly psycho-dynamic reading of the OB she finds, with a cognitive one. She attributes the OB, in part, to information processing problems: 'generic men and one's own man are held in mind separately so that *cognitive processes do not bring them into contact* and expose their similar tendencies' (Sobo, 1995: 118, my italics). She adds a notion of a hierarchy of risk in which her respondents operate: the benefit of unsafe sex outweighs the risks taken if one were to ask for safer sex, which may include verbal abuse, physical abuse, loss of the partner and childlessness with loss of self-esteem and financial hardship being possible consequences of these. Sobo also finds that condom-use decisions are related to emotional and socio-historical factors: women who are less dependent on men for self-esteem and support are less likely to forgo condoms.

A number of other empirical studies in the AIDS field corroborate the 'unrealistically' low assessment of risk among those who epidemiologists deem to be at high risk. In a large study of British drug users, Stimson *et al.* (1988) show that while 36 per cent had recently shared needles, only 7 per cent perceived themselves to be at risk of contracting HIV. In prisons, where the weight of evidence suggests a higher than average rate of HIV seroprevalence, prisoners rate their risk of getting HIV/AIDS as higher for others than themselves, whether they are inside or outside prison, and rate their risk inside prison as lower than that outside (Markova *et al.*, 1995).

In a meta-analysis of AIDS-related studies on OB, Gerrard *et al.* (1996) indicate that social, emotional and other factors, rather than cognitive perceptions of vulnerability alone, determine precautionary sexual behaviour. They go as far as to propose that 'it could be that the more affective components of perceptions of vulnerability, rather than the cognitive representation of likelihood, are the critical motivators of precaution adoption' (Gerrard *et al.*, 1996: 405). Many researchers in the OB area continue to make inappropriate assumptions about the rationality of the lone thinker despite evidence, published in the most esteemed of journals, which questions this vision.

Attribution theory: the 'not me' response, intentionality and blame

The OB tradition has a long history. Eschewing one's own links to negative events has been theorised by one of the most established approaches within social psychology: attribution theory (AT). The attribution process may underpin the underestimation of personal risk, when making comparisons with others (Weinstein, 1980). Attribution theory is a cognitive theory of how people judge the causes of events. Since my concern is with lay explanations of crises, I shall draw on those aspects of AT that address this issue.

A major error that people make when explaining the cause of an event is to hold an egocentric illusion: the cause of positive events is attributed to the self, and of negative events, to others (Kelley, 1973). This may be translatable into an ethnocentric bias: that people attribute positive events to their own group and negative events to other groups. Augmenting this, the 'fundamental attributional error' (Ross, 1977) occurs. Those operating within this attributional style overestimate the role of dispositional factors, and underestimate the role of situational factors in their explanations of the negative events that befall other people. Others, rather than oneself, are more likely to have caused negative events and their behaviour or their character, rather than a situation they found themselves in, is linked with the cause. Since the cause of the event which befalls the other lies in what is perceived to be the controllable element (i.e. dispositional rather than situational factors), human intention is implicated. Since we hold others more responsible for actions that are perceived to be intentional, than those that are seen to arise from unintended sources (Heider, 1958), high levels of personal responsibility are placed with others who are linked to the negative event. In fact, the extent of responsibility assigned *increases* as the consequences of the negative event are perceived as more serious (Walster, 1966). When faced with the task of making sense of risks, people are likely to link volitional others to them, thereby protecting themselves from the thought that this type of misfortune might happen to anyone, including themselves.

Approached from a slightly different angle, later models (e.g. Weiner,

1980) posit that when faced with people in a plight, perceivers attempt to determine its cause. If it is attributed to uncontrollable factors, sympathy results. This is currently manifest in the division between people who get AIDS through blood products, heterosexual sex and mother–infant transmission, rather than out-groups who get it. Otherwise, a negative emotional response ensues. The greater the perceived freedom of control over the actions which lead to the event, the greater the blame assigned. When extended to a disaster, the overriding tendency is to feel little sympathy and to give high culpability ratings, unless the victims or relevant authorities could not have stopped it by way of good judgement (Russell and Mentzel, 1990). Since people are likely to be perceived as intentional, volitional creatures, the assignment of fault is the likely outcome when the causes of their misfortunes are explained.

The vast majority of the studies cited in elucidating both OB and AT are carried out on Western samples. When researchers conduct cross-cultural assessments of attribution, a more varied picture arises. In evaluating the OB model, I indicated that more emphasis upon self-control may be involved in Western, as opposed to non-Western, comparative risk judgements. Westerners tend to see misfortunes as more controllable than others do (e.g. Kleinhesselink and Rosa, 1991). The need for mastery, competence and superiority seems to be linked to perceptions of heightened control (Langer, 1975). This finds resonance in the broader social scientific work on the way that Western culture has accrued its positive identity. It has done so by contrasting its values to those of 'others', who are deemed to have less self-control, and therefore to be inferior beings. The massive emphasis upon control over one's destiny is quite particular to societies pervaded by the ideology of individualism. This, together with the attribution tradition, was anticipated in a succinct line of reasoning put forward by the social psychologist Gustav Ichheiser some time ago:

The misinterpretations which consist in underestimating the importance of situational and in overestimating the importance of personal factors do not arise by chance. *These misinterpretations are not personal errors committed by ignorant individuals.* They are, rather, a *consistent and inevitable consequence of the social system and of the ideology of the nineteenth century,* which led us to believe that our fate in the social space depended exclusively, or at least predominantly, on our individual qualities – that we, as individuals, and not the prevailing social conditions, shape our lives. (Ichheiser, 1943:152, original italics)

This argument is particularly useful in that it provides a clear indication that judgements can be shaped primarily by ideological forces, rather than by cognitive errors of judgement. In late modern societies individuals are assumed, increasingly, to engineer the consequences which befall them. Consequently, becoming the victim of a disaster is represented as having a self-procured element. With self-control, people can avoid negative outcomes. It is highly plausible that the cultural idea that individuals are entities who are responsible for the outcomes which befall them, in Western societies, explains why the 'fundamental attribution error' occurs (see Farr, 1987).

The growing emphasis on people shaping their destinies by way of volitional acts (rather than genetic heritage, constitution and chance playing a role) has been carefully theorised in the field of health and illness. There have been explicit statements concerning a belief in self-control over health from those in charge of the health of nations in Western countries. For example, in the 1970s, Britain's Department of Health and Social Security's (1976) position paper stated that: 'Modern western diseases are related less to a man's environment than to his own personal behaviour; what might be termed "our lifestyle"' (1976:17). Similarly, the US Surgeon-General's report in 1979 concluded that the chief causes of illness lie in individual behaviour (Nelkin and Gilman, 1988). Evidence for such declarations was rather tenuous. Crawford (1977) assessed the causes of cancer, for example, and concluded that 70–90 per cent of cancers are environmentally caused. However, increasingly, cancer has become linked, in popular consciousness, to individual irresponsibility in terms of adopting an unhealthy lifestyle. More recently, variations in health have been linked to socio-economic factors. For example, mortality rates in Britain are linked to social class (see Pitts, 1996). Furthermore, Wilkinson (1996) shows that the larger the gap between rich and poor, the lower the average life expectancy is in Western societies. Inequality, with the attendant lack of social cohesiveness, rather than lifestyle choices, may be a key determinant of health.

The assumption that illness arises from inappropriate behaviours easily slides into the view that illness reflects personal failing. 'Being ill' is redefined as 'being guilty'. Ill people are assumed to have been aware of the repercussions of their illness-producing actions and consequently can be blamed for their illnesses. The new developments in the discernment of genes which predispose people to illness throw up interesting challenges to the choice ethos, at least in the sphere of health risks.

Self-control is intricately tied in with choice. A cultural influence upon the attribution of personal responsibility for crises relates to the Western assumption that people possess freedom of action, freedom to choose. Yet the capacity to choose and the opportunity to do so are quite different things (Doyal and Harris, 1986). Variants of coercion, such as those evident in Sobo's (1995) findings (see pp. 62–63), among other factors, hinder the capacity to make choices. The distinction between the capacity and opportunity to choose is particularly important in the face of a range of crises in which external constraints can impair opportunities to make safe choices.

Since control and choice are perceived to be at the heart of people's actions in Western societies, people can be held responsible for the outcomes that befall them: chance or external pressures are not generally allocated a key role. The victim of a mass threat is often blamed for bringing about the ill fortune. When Lerner (1980) coined the term 'just world hypothesis' he was drawing together the early attributional work cited above. The 'just world hypothesis' proposes that people believe that the plight of other people is deserved. It casts the world in such a way as 'good people' are rewarded with 'good' consequences, and 'bad people', with 'bad' consequences. All is fair. The next step is punishment: a major motive for attribution of responsibility is to censure people who are associated with the cause of the misfortune. The need to find a culprit relates to the need to prevent the misfortune from recurring. Once responsibility has been established, the misfortune can be avenged. Vengeance may appear in symbolic forms such as in metaphors and jokes which associate the crisis with certain groups and practices, or in acts of violence. In the case of AIDS, the gamut of responses has ranged from 'gay plague' metaphors to 'gay bashing'. The seeking out of culprits who may, because of their actions, be deemed responsible for the misfortune, also relates to a need for determinacy. Once a culprit is chosen, responsibility and blame can be determined.

Certain theorists who work within this cognitive paradigm worry about the conceptual confusion which has entered into work on the attribution of blame. Shaver and Drown (1986), in particular, are concerned that causality, responsibility and blameworthiness be held as conceptually different entities, rather than being used interchangeably, as they sometimes are in the attributions literature. They offer a number of examples in which lay people accept that there is a distinction between these three entities. People are able to hold a man responsible for failing to prevent a misfortune such as a burglary, without believing that he caused it. Similarly, people may believe that a woman's own behaviour was linked with the cause of her rape, without blaming her for being raped. Shaver and Drown (1986) propose a model in which judgements of causality, responsibility and blame are interlinked but nevertheless distinct. This distinction may be important in relation to responses at times of crisis: if a person is thought to be in some way responsible for an untoward outcome, it does not follow directly that blame in relation to causality is present. However, convincing empirical work indicates that blame is accompanied by the belief that another person caused, or was in some way responsible for, an untoward outcome (Tennen and Affleck, 1990). Intent and volition are also implied when blame is present.

The cognitivist emphasis in AT can be subject to the same critique as that in the OB literature. The cognitive underpinnings imply a deluded, error-prone individual without taking heed of the influence of culture. Western assumptions concerning the responsible and volitional nature of individuals, coupled with a great fear of indeterminacy, influences the process whereby bad events are dumped onto 'others' who are held responsible for them. However, the cultural argument must be pursued with great caution, and requires considerable further investigation. Although self-control appears to be more valued in Western contexts, and a blaming attributional style follows from this, I have shown, in chapters 2 and 3, that the tendency to associate good events with the self and in-group, and bad events with 'others', extends beyond purely Western contexts.

The OB and AT traditions suggest highly complementary motives. Attribution work has taken its cue from Heider's early work which highlights the meaning-making motivation: when people observe others, they are especially concerned with their motives, since this gives meaning to what it experienced. The more threatening the event, the more it demands an explanation, so that people are able to create a sense of meaning (see Tennen and Affleck, 1990). In general, volitional acts, rather than external environmental factors, are linked with misfortunes. This allows for a sense of determinacy, thereby allaying fears that one's chances of striking misfortune contain a random quality. The emphasis on control is also present in the overestimation of one's skills to deal with the risk, which is a key explanation of what underpins OB. The similarity of the motives which underpin OB and AT is hardly surprising since the AT tradition precedes, and runs alongside, the OB tradition within mainstream social psychology.

Optimism's effects on physical and mental health

Optimism can be highly useful in the face of the possibility of being affected by a crisis. Research which explores the links between optimism and physical and mental health detects strong links between optimism and mental and physical health. The 'not me – others' response to adverse events leaves people psychologically and physically more healthy than those who see their chances of becoming affected in realistic terms

(see Taylor and Armor, 1996). Mental health rests on illusions, especially exaggerated perceptions of personal control and OB (Taylor and
Brown, 1988). Recent evidence points to a further advantage of optimism: those who are optimistically biased have more T cells, which
mediate immune reactions to infection, as well as higher natural killer
cell cytotoxicity which is believed to be important in mediating immunity to viral infection and to certain types of cancer (Segerstrom *et al.*,
1998). Optimism, tied to better physical health and better psychological
coping, may produce these effects through its impact upon the immune
system. While immune improvements provide a fascinating angle on the
link between optimism and health-related issues, they obviously have
little consequence for non-health-related risks. The very emphasis and
study of the effects of optimism has produced interesting findings at the
biological level, but it remains fascinating that these findings fit so well
with the ideology of the societies in which they are explored: higher
levels of positive thinking regarding one's future equates with higher
levels of physical and psychological health.

It is important to note that while optimism can be functional at a
biological level, it may open people to physical vulnerability. At the core
of the Health Belief Model (Maiman and Becker, 1974) lies the assumption that perceived vulnerability plays a vital role in health protective
behaviour. If people do not see themselves as vulnerable to a health or
safety risk, they may be unlikely to act to prevent themselves from being
affected by the danger. A sense of bravado in relation to being affected
by a war, a hurricane or an earthquake may diminish one's worry about
it affecting one, yet it may also reduce one's chances of taking precautions in relation to the danger.

Concluding remarks

In this chapter I explored two strands of the cognitive literature on the
optimistic appraisal of risks, and examined the factors that might
underpin this phenomenon. The scope and limitations of cognitive
models of the response to risks were assessed. I highlighted the inability
of purely cognitive models to explore the latent cultural and emotional
contours of the 'not me – other' response. The value dimension is also
absent from such models.

The findings which emerge from the OB and AT paradigms are very
similar to those of my own empirical work (see chapter 3) and of the
social scientific work on responses to crises (see chapter 2). People tend
to distance themselves from risks and to imagine that others are more
likely than they are to be affected. The robust nature of this finding is

reinforced by the different angles and methods which have been used to establish it. In the case of OB, in general, scales are used to establish how respondents compare themselves to their peers in relation to an array of risks, and to rate other factors concerning the risks, such as their perceived severity. AT studies tend to be based upon experiments which present respondents with hypothetical scenarios in relation to which they are asked to make judgements. These methods can be juxtaposed with the more 'real-world' nature of interview-based methods, and with the analyses of texts and images utilised by historians and cultural theorists who study responses to crises. This triangulation, in approach and in method, provides strong validation for the phenomenon.

It is at the level of explaining *why* the 'not me – others' response occurs in the face of potential crises that more complex theorisation must be introduced. There is a need to discern factors that underpin this response which go beyond those offered by cognitive psychologists. This is not important solely in theoretical terms. The relationship between perceived vulnerability and precautionary behaviour is a key component in virtually all contemporary models of health-protective behaviour (Gerrard *et al.*, 1996). Perceived vulnerability tends to be seen as a primary motivation for avoidance of risky behaviour and the initiation of precautionary behaviour. These models underpin major governmental attempts to improve the health of nations.

The poverty of purely cognitive explanations is demonstrated by continued bafflement in the face of risk-taking behaviour, on the part of researchers and practitioners steeped in these ideas. Health promotion based on cognitive premises has a vision of a rational, lone individual making cognitive errors, in a value-free environment. These assumptions are particularly problematic in the face of risks which involve a high level of emotional and physical arousal (such as unsafe sex) and chemical changes in the body (such as alcohol and drug-related risks). In fact, one might argue that since risks are often linked with excitement and desire, the more rational faculties of the mind are not to the fore in the decision-making that surrounds them. Furthermore, risks often take place in the presence of others, and in sexually related risks in particular, negotiation rather than lone decisions will determine whether safer practices occur. By locating risk-related thinking in the minds of individuals, cognitively led research and intervention programmes fail to tap the dynamic interaction between the social context and individual minds. They also fail to take non-conscious motivations into consideration. These include tacit cultural and unconscious psycho-dynamic forces. This omission is not surprising since mainstream psychology, which is characterised by these cognitive models, is currently predominantly a science of the conscious mind (Moscovici, 1982; Markova and Wilkie, 1987).

One of the key claims of this book is that perceptions of misfortune in a society are not based purely upon probability ratings. The history of epidemiology and of government responses to epidemiologically identified risks is not just a rational one in which the worst risks get the most attention and funding. Far from being a neutral concept, grounded in probabilistic data, danger, veiled under the modern concept of 'risk', is used as a strategy for identifying villains and victims and for casting blame for unwelcome events. The beliefs cherished by a culture or segment thereof – and because of this stable over time – enter into thinking about misfortunes. The values of a society are brought to the fore via the exaggeration of risks such as AIDS, and the underestimation of risks which are more difficult to link to moral issues, such as the risk of cancer from the sun. By playing up the spectre of AIDS, sexual relations can be regulated so that they conform to the traditional family values which a society finds advantageous. Debates about misfortunes are debates about moral and political concerns, rather than purely about the material risks faced by people. The way that risk is read does not rest purely upon individual cognitive faculties. Risk is also comprehended in accordance with the relationship between the self and the community (Douglas, 1992).

A wider conceptualisation of risk must be forged, ensuring that findings are grounded in empirical data. There is a need to introduce a broader focus into an approach on how individuals respond to potential crises. The focus on the individual-embedded-in-culture-and-society is lacking in most work on the apprehension of risks. Work on risk assessment tends to focus either on the cognition of the individual, or on the community consensus and solidarity which can result from responses to risks. In certain respect this book is a project in keeping with that of Henriques *et al.* (1984/1998) in which there is an endeavour to bring together the social and the subjective elements of human experience. This focus is extremely important for the risk area, not least because risk-preventive interventions that fail to take the we-embedded-in-the-I into account are doomed to fail.

I have shown that while the weight of data that exist on the human response to threat certainly points to a widespread 'not me' response, explanations of what underpins this requires a different emphasis. Subsequent chapters focus on a set of assumptions which conceive of the human as an emotional creature who views risks through a culturally tinged lens. Cognitive 'errors' are construed as defences upon which people's positive sense of identity rests.

NOTES

1 While the issue of preventability is most salient in the literature, Weinstein (1987) shows that three other beliefs determine the amount of OB elicited: the belief that if a problem has not yet appeared, one is exempt from future risk; lack of experience with the hazard makes it appear unlikely that one will be affected by it; the perception that the hazard is infrequent leads one to dismiss the likelihood of it affecting oneself. Langer (1975) suggests that humans are not always able to discriminate between controllable and uncontrollable events. This is linked to skill and chance being closely associated in people's experience: there is an element of chance in every skill situation and an element of skill in many chance situations. Rather than being motivated to read control into situations, people may have real difficulty in discriminating between pure chance and pure skill situations because these rarely exist.

2 There is some controversy in this regard. Budescu and Bruderman (1995) show, experimentally, that having a sense of control and having a 'rosy picture' of one's current or future risks are influenced by different factors. People consistently paint a 'rosy picture' of events that will befall them, irrespective of the degree of control they feel they have over the event being predicted. The tendency to paint a 'rosy picture' exists in the absence of illusions of control. However, these authors recognise that their study is based on hypothetical rather than 'real-life' risks, and that this may influence their results.

5   The source of linking risk and 'the other': splitting objects into 'good' and 'bad'

Having presented evidence for the existence of the 'not me – others are to blame' response across a range of disasters in various cultures, this is the first of the two chapters that set out my framework for understanding blaming responses with regard to potential crises. It draws on psycho-dynamic, social psychological and socio-cultural theories, assessing their compatibility. Anxiety and the response to it are its organising concepts.

Splitting: the origin of the 'not me – others' phenomenon

The origin of the attempt to protect the identity of the self by linking threatening events with 'the other' has been carefully explored by psycho-dynamic theorists. With notable exceptions, their focus has not been on responses to mass risks but their theories are well suited to this area. In particular, I utilise the work of the British object relations theorist Melanie Klein in conjunction with certain Freudian tenets to understand the source of the 'not me – others' phenomenon.[1]

Melanie Klein's work on people's earliest mental operations provides considerable insight into adult responses to threat. A composite portrait of the Kleinian view of the infant's experience will be charted, highlighting those aspects which play a part in shaping responses to potential crises in later life. The primary focus is on the unconscious defence termed 'splitting' which is an essential aspect of a theory of the representation of threat. Splitting is a way of viewing the world in simplistic terms by seeing it as either black or white. A middle ground is missing when one splits. The roots of the splitting process lie in the earliest moments of infancy. In Kleinian theory anxiety is an organising concept and splitting is a response to early anxiety. The psyche develops from affective roots. From birth the infant experiences anxiety. The maturing process revolves around strengthening and organising the self against this anxiety.[2] From the earliest stages of infancy mental operations such as splitting which reduce anxiety are brought into play, to ensure a sense of safety and security for the maturing being.

The first step in the infant's maturation process is the paranoid-schizoid position (Klein, 1946, 1952). It is important to note that the term 'position' rather than 'stage' or 'phase' is used to designate that the anxieties and defences which constitute this position are not restricted to the first year of the infant's life but recur throughout life (Doane and Hodges, 1992). This is particularly relevant for my approach, which aims to discern the roots of adult responses to threats. The first position begins in the early moments of life which are characterised by inter-action with the 'primary object', which is generally the mother.[3] A crucial aspect of this model is that it places this relationship at the root of mental life. Thinking begins in a social relationship.

The infant's early interaction with the mother is both gratifying and frustrating, both 'good' and 'bad'. Satisfaction, rather than frustration, depends on the ability of the mother to fathom or to respond to all of the infant's needs. At times when its needs are fulfilled, the infant experiences the mother as satisfying and loving. When its needs are not fulfilled, it experiences its mother as persecutory. When the infant experiences persecution, such as when the mother does not provide sustenance, feelings of aggression, hate and destruction are evoked. Destructive feelings are accompanied by feelings of extreme anxiety. The infant is paranoid that destructive forces are motivated to harm it. The infant does not merely endure these feelings. Infants appear to be orientated towards maintaining their experience of nurturance, satisfac-tion, safety and security. Mechanisms are put to work to ward off the anxiety induced by the perceived threat of persecution. Paranoid feelings are dispensed with by separating them off from the loving feelings which the infant seeks to retain. Splitting, an unconscious mechanism of defence, is generally associated with taking into the self good experi-ences and feelings, and the projection outward of bad experiences and feelings. Freud suggests that 'the bodily prototype for spitting out bad-tasting objects serves as a template for the primitive psychic defence called splitting' (see Sloan, 1996: 71).

The point of splitting is to keep the bad away from the good in the hope that it will not invade the good and destroy it. The key factor is that this mechanism sustains a lack of integration of the opposite poles of feeling, within the infant: one side of the infant's experience is all good, and the other all bad. Each set of experiences is kept separate in the infant's mind. The two poles are available to the infant only as alternatives.

Freud's bodily prototype for splitting provides a useful image. Yet

Klein is more concerned with the mechanism of putting bad things outside of the self at the *level of representation* than in a bodily way. Klein rarely focuses on the bodily interaction between the mother and infant. Instead she highlights the infant's phantasies concerning the mother (Doane and Hodges, 1992). Thus she is centrally concerned with early representation formation, in the mind of the infant and this makes her work particularly relevant for a theory of the symbolisation of threats. In this earliest phase of life, the infant holds a split representation of the world. Bad experiences and objects tend to be placed outside of the self, while the infant clings to good experiences, not wanting to sully them. My framework for the human response to risk holds the residues of this split, early representation of the world as a key feature. The split representation contains 'the glorious moral certainties and simplicities of the comic strip and the nursery story, of all the goodies versus baddies stories that delight and relieve and reassure children' (Temperley, 1989: 261).

One may ask why this process does not work in reverse. If the prime motivation is to keep good and bad apart, why not introject the bad and project the good? This can occur. Yet it is less typical and it is for this reason that spitting out bad tasting objects is a useful metaphor for the concept. A key tenet of Freud's work, the life force, is crucial if we are to understand the proclivity towards projection of bad outwards and towards introjection of the good. Freud attests to the primacy of the body's drive to maximise pleasure and to minimise pain, in the early structuring of the psyche (see Sloan, 1996). Adherence to a life force and rejection of destructive impulses provide the seeds of an explanation for the psyche's orientation towards identification with positive experiences. Early representational activity protects a positive inner space. It also allows the self to begin to discern order in the world, by separating experiences from one another. It is in this first paranoid-schizoid position that the roots of an ability to order chaos are laid (Allingham, 1987).

Beyond the forces of projection and introjection, Klein and her followers develop the notion of projective identification to characterise a more complex dynamic that occurs in the paranoid-schizoid position.[4] This construct is particularly relevant for theories concerned with the location of threat within 'the other'. Projective identification means not only that parts of the self which one does not want to own are projected into external objects, but also that these external objects are then seen to be possessed by, controlled by and identified with the projected parts. The objects onto which people project their aggression become feared as a source of belligerence (Frosh, 1989b; Moses, 1989). The aim in projective processes is not only to rid the self of 'bad' parts, but also, crucially, to be able to control the source of danger. Yet this does not get accomplished since the material that one gets rid of becomes feared. I have explored the way in which the 'other' becomes debased at times of crisis (see chapter 2). Outsiders are forced to carry qualities from which insiders seek to distance themselves, in order to sustain a sense of orderliness. Yet rather than gaining a firm sense of comfort from this process, insiders find outsiders terribly threatening since they become associated with the polluting, contaminating qualities ascribed to them. The bad qualities that the outsiders are left to carry threaten to 'leak' back into the space of the insiders. This is vividly illustrated in social representations of AIDS in which leakage from 'the other' into the pure space of the 'general public' has been a key anxiety, and is reflected in the earliest government preventive campaigns (see chapter 3).

What further insights can a theory which elucidates the development of the stark divorcing of 'bad' objects from 'good', in the early years, offer a theory of adult responses to disasters? A key emphasis of the Kleinian outlook is that humans do not merely resolve one position and move onto another, in the maturation process. Rather, a position leaves a residue on the developing human and all humans can be plunged back into operating as if they were in one of the early positions, in later life. When changes in the social environment make for insecurity, a strong sense of anxiety is evoked. Representations such as the 'sin cocktail', which manifests in initial, adult responses to AIDS (see chapter 3), are forms of this early representational activity, an activity in which 'the other' can be fantasised in terms of one's own 'bad' thoughts. The early pattern of representation which allows the infant to handle anxiety is reproduced: 'the first ways of relating to objects are never forgotten, nor completely replaced' (Allingham, 1987: 33). The first ways of relating to others are instilled in the patterns of adult social representations.

Anthropological insights concerning the orientation towards 'the other' at times of raised anxiety are similar to Kleinian ideas. This compatibility is surprising since anthropological insights do not locate the roots of such responses in infancy. They tend to utilise ethnographic methods, as opposed to the clinical methods of research used by Klein. The anthropological insights of Lévi-Strauss (1967) emphasise the mind's need for order. Order is achieved by placing everything of which the mind is aware into fixed categories. The internal 'logic' of this process lies in what is appropriate in each culture. Mary Douglas also develops her theory on the basis of a mind which seeks order. According to Douglas (1966), people construct symbolic systems of purity – analogous to spaces of 'goodness' in psycho-dynamic terms – so as to order what they experience as the chaotic set of stimuli which surround them. Those elements that threaten the order of the system, such as potential disasters, are classified to be outside of the system. They are regarded as potentially polluting in that they can cross over into the order – the 'goodness' – and destroy it. One can switch seamlessly between such insights and psychodynamic findings. Grounded in a complementary psychoanalytic perspective Phillips (1995) points out: 'If the aim of a system is to create an outside where you can put the things you don't want, then we have to look at what that system disposes of – its rubbish – to understand it, to get a picture of how it sees itself and wants to be seen' (Phillips, 1995: 19). This statement provides strong grounds for doing interview-based research in which people structure their own accounts of potential threats. In people's talk we find indications of what they wish to distance themselves from, and of how they represent the pure inner space inhabited by their in-group and self. Furthermore, Phillips' statement demonstrates that one can move between strands of psychoanalytically and anthropologically grounded work on disasters, making similar assertions. The point made in this statement is also highly complementary with the claim, made by cultural theorists such as Said (see chapter 2), that the way that a group defines the 'other' discloses how it defines itself.

Douglas' claims concerning the response to crises, in particular, bear remarkable similarity to those of Klein, both in terms of the nature of the contents of the response and in terms of being universalist: all people have the tendency to split good from bad spaces and to cling to the good space, especially at times of raised anxiety. The two approaches are noteworthy for their divergence from social psychological work which locates the motivation to protect self-esteem, to locate 'bad' outside of the self, in the Western, individualist tradition. Farr's (1977) work advances this social psychological notion: he points to a number of empirical inquiries such as Herzlich's (1973) study of representations of health and illness, and claims that a specifically Western ethos accounts for the tendency to associate that which is outside the individual with negative states, and to align the self with positive outcomes. The mainstream psychological research in this area (see chapter 4) also favours such cultural differences. However, the evidence from the risk literatures which I have presented proposes a more universalist set of responses. It points to the symmetry between Western and non-Western representations. This commonality may relate to a universal life force which leads to the preservation of a good inner space. This does not preclude the possibility that cultures build particular influences into these responses. Perhaps the 'inner space' refers to *individuals* in Western cultures, while it relates to the *in-group* and to one's own *community* in less individualist cultures. Furthermore, there appears to be a pattern which is particular to the contemporary Western reaction to crises, in which crises are ascribed quite directly to 'bad' *human agents* (see Herzlich and Pierret, 1987), rather than to other forces such as gods or spirits.

I have shown that the Kleinian model is remarkably useful in terms of positing the origin of the tendency to represent others in polarised terms, as either all 'good' or all 'bad'. For Klein, traces of this early pattern of representation exist in all people, though in variable degrees. While Klein refers to the infant's orientation towards maintaining a sense of security, comfort and safety, in line with the Freudian life force, her work is generally associated with an overemphasis of the negative, paranoid and destructive nature of the infant. This issue is somewhat equivocal. Klein's work does seem to indicate that as a function of the life force, people attempt to protect the 'good' facets of themselves and others by splitting the 'good' from the 'bad' and projecting the 'bad' outside of the self. However, her theory also posits a strong sense of paranoia and of destructive impulses. Projection onto 'the other', who thereby becomes imbued with dangerous qualities, magnifies the sense of paranoia invoked in the projector, in the paranoid-schizoid position. Paranoia is accompanied by destructive feelings.

One further facet of the Kleinian explanation of early mental processing contributes to an explanatory framework for responses to crises. She posits that blurred boundaries exist between the self and others in the earliest months of life. Since the boundary between the individual's 'self' and the primary object is highly volatile at this stage, outside objects are easily seen as possessing qualities which belong to the self, and self is easily seen as possessing qualities which belong to others. An understanding that there is a state in which humans are unaware of where they end and others begin is useful for a theory of response to risk. A state in which one is oblivious to a difference between the space of the self and that of outside objects or people is one in which thoughts and feelings can float around without being linked to one or other party: 'an essential ingredient of the social network is that bits of experience, affects, emotions, feeling-states, are moved around. These channels of unconscious, non-conscious communication are separate from, but intertwined with, the verbal and cognitive communication' (Hinshelwood, 1989b:77). The projective process indicates that, unconsciously, people use the social context as a means of passing on to others certain feeling states, particularly elements of themselves which they wish to disown.

The combination of aspects of the Kleinian and Freudian models which I present offers a major asset to theorisation of the social aspects of responses to threats. This stands in contrast to the charge that psycho-dynamic theory's concern is solely with intra-subjective experiences. From infancy to later life, when faced with anxiety provoking situations, there is a rearrangement in people's representations of themselves and of others. People organise their representations in accordance with the struggle for a sense of a boundary between a pure inner space, and a polluted, outside world. The subjective management of anxiety springs from a *relational* process in which the self continuously strives for protection from negative feelings evoked in it by dumping unwanted material onto 'others' at the level of representation. Holding certain and not other representations, in relation to threatening phenomena, relates to a self-protective motivation.

Psycho-dynamic theory and socio-historical processes

Kleinian psycho-dynamic concepts provide the seeds of an explanation of the origin and role of social interaction and representational activity in the human response to threat. One facet of this response is the finding of an 'other' who can become the target of one's unwanted thoughts, allowing one to place them outside of the boundaries of the self. In Kleinian terms, anxiety, and the representations that form around it, spring from a social relationship: that between the infant and the mother's body (Klein, 1929). Despite this social focus, even the more macro-social variants of Kleinian theory do not account for the link between early relations and socio-historical processes. Used alone, Kleinian theory does not account for how (or which) social forces exacerbate or allay splitting in the adult. The salience of the groups with which people affiliate, and their fundamental role in the formation of the individual's representational structures, is not captured. A key aim of the chapter is to show how psycho-dynamic and social theory can be utilised in a complementary way, in order to understand subjective responses to risks.

There is a body of psychodynamically driven data which attests to the mirroring of individual processes in group situations. Bion (1952, 1961), Jaques (1977), Kaes (1980) and Hinshelwood (1987) have shown how early 'splitting' becomes a part of interaction in therapeutic groups. Segal (1995) has shown how it is evident in political groups, and Menzies-Lyth (1960, 1989) how it is at work among nurses in hospitals. This corpus of studies corroborates the mechanism used to deal with anxiety posited by Klein and her followers. It shows that these different types of groups act as a safety net, containing anxiety for their individual members, by helping them to project anxiety outward onto others. This body of research deals with actual groups of people. One unifying feature of these studies is that they focus on 'real' interactions in group situations, such as the nursing system ensuring that the considerable anxiety of nurses is diminished by eliminating situations which evoke anxiety. More salient in the response of individuals to mass crises are groups-in-the-mind, groups with which individuals identify symbolically in expressing their stance in relation to various phenomena, but who do not actually gather together in any material sense. Prominent social scientists such as Serge Moscovici identify the sense in which one can belong to groups without having any material contact with them:

the media penetrate every home and seek out every individual to change him into a member of a mass . . . It is the kind of mass, however, that is seen nowhere because it is everywhere. The millions of people who quietly read their paper and involuntarily talk like their radio are members of the new kind of crowd . . . They stay at home, but they are all together, and all seem different, but are similar. (Moscovici, 1985:193)

The emphasis upon the mass media is particularly important in the examination of mass responses to disasters, since most individuals hear about potential disasters via this medium. The individual who I study shares many fundamental beliefs and feelings with others, without necessarily participating in any formal group situations with them.

It is important to go beyond pointing to the parallel individual and 'real group' processes of splitting, to address the mediation between individual and societal processes of defence. I turn to discerning how the representations held by individuals become permeated with group-specific expressions of affiliation and protection, in the course of the lifespan. Social Identity Theory (SIT) provides a key link in the transition from the intra-individual to the inter-group level of thought. A conclusive set of experimental results in this field vouches for the link between individual and group processes. SIT provides strong evidence that social identities, such as racial and gender identities, form a part of personal identity (Tajfel and Turner, 1979). In the course of identifying with a group, the need to perceive oneself positively, on the inter-individual level, translates into a need to regard one's group favourably. In the process of forming a personal identity, affinities are forged with certain group identities in the social environment. Certain groups are integrated into the 'good' self and become one's in-groups while others are construed as the 'bad' other, and become one's out-groups.

The social cognitive SIT can be used to produce an explanation for how intra-individual splitting gains a social counterpart: splitting 'good' from 'bad' objects with the aim of protection of the self may extend to forging a category system concerning which groups are 'good' and which are 'bad'. However, caution must be exercised in positing that individuals identify with a fixed set of groups and view their in-groups as pure, and their out-groups as potentially dangerous. The notion of fixed group identifications has been challenged. Identity is a shifting entity (e.g. see Greenwood, 1994). Being black, for example, does not necessarily fix a person to a particular set of affiliations since in most societies there are no structural features to ensure that identity is formed or maintained in line with this type of group. Moreover, the theory also has limited explanatory power in relation to responses to crises since it emphasises the *process* of inter-group affiliation, rather than the *content* of thinking. It verifies for us where identification is likely to lie, but not what mental representations will be created when faced with having to think about an event, such as a crisis.

It is the latter criticism, in particular, that drives me to incorporate theories that lie beyond the realm of social cognition. In this chapter I draw on common threads in the work of psycho-dynamically orientated socio-cultural theorists (Sherwood, 1980; Gilman, 1985a, 1988; Andreski, 1989) to account for how socio-historical factors impact upon the contents of individuals' responses to threat. In chapter 6 I consolidate this strand of thought within a social representational paradigm.

Change in the social environment, such as the rising presence of a mass risk, is one of the ways in which anxiety is evoked within people. Such changes make for insecurity which exacerbates people's early splitting defence. In the face of a mass crisis, in which people perceive their world to be out of control, with their protection compromised, representations which contain an element of inter-group projection are most likely to arise. The crucial point is that factors within the individual's social environment either activate or constrain the individual's use of defence mechanisms such as projection (Sherwood, 1980). Firstly, events in the social environment, which get portrayed as particularly threatening, activate defence mechanisms. Had AIDS, for example, been depicted in a less menacing way, protection via projection may not have been so crucial to those who needed to understand the new phenomenon. Secondly, the extent to which it is permissible to project onto certain groups is regulated by the social order. Each individual enters a world of existing representations, a world in which certain groups have already been represented as respectable and others as degenerate. Representations which circulate in a particular social group, prior to the individual's entry into it, influence who and what the individual chooses as the representative of the 'bad other', onto whom anxiety-provoking feelings can be projected. Each social group has various 'repositories' (Sherwood, 1980) who are often 'defenceless groups' (Gilman, 1988; Andreski, 1989) which it stores as potential targets for its projection. Certain groups have repeatedly represented the 'bad other' within certain societies:

> Every social group has a set vocabulary of images for this externalized Other. These images are the product of history and of a culture that perpetuates them. None is random; none is isolated from the historical context. From the wide range of the potential models in any society, we select a model that best reflects the common presuppositions about the other at any given moment in history. (Gilman, 1985a:20)

The AIDS-related blaming and conspiracy theories (see chapter 3) demonstrate that different groups in a society have very different 'repositories' for their defensive projections. In the early years of the epidemic, members of marginalised groups tended to link AIDS with the malevolent conspiracies of Western scientists, while members of more dominant groups linked it with marginalised groups. I have pointed out that these symmetrical accusations do not rest upon equal footings. The dominant ideologies within a society tend to propagate an image of specific groups as the entire society's 'other'. For example, I have shown that in the nineteenth century, black women and prostitutes were the repositories for projections related to syphilis in the West, and 'the poor' for those related to cholera and typhus in Britain. A number of theorists, particularly psycho-dynamically based thinkers, believe that one can uncover universal tenets for which groups will become 'the other'. Kristeva (1991) posits that going back in history, and moving across myriad societies, the key 'others' have been those who lie outside of the family, the clan, the tribe and sometimes of the religion. With the founding of the nation-state, 'the other' is one who does not belong to the state. Gilman (1988) has posited universal features in the content of what these 'others' are imbued with. He claims that inferior racial identity and sexual perversion are fairly universally ascribed to 'the other'.

Freud's bodily metaphor for projection of bad outward, spitting out bad-tasting food, becomes layered with wider social and moral connotations as the infant grows up. Disgust is a key element in this process. Research on disgust, from a non-psycho-dynamic perspective, shows that disgust relates to rejection of what is felt to be potentially contaminated or distasteful either physically or psychologically (Strongman, 1996). It appears to occur as a direct bodily reaction. Yet people also learn to be disgusted in the course of their development, from what they are told is disgusting: putting sand in one's mouth is not disgusting for babies, but the growing child learns that it is from parents. Izard (1991) points out that feeling disgusted by someone is usually accompanied by contempt for that person, with the consequent feelings of superiority. Disgust appears to be particularly bound up with the moral order and is inculcated via socialisation rather than containing a purely material, bodily source. Disgust and contempt concerning certain 'others' have their roots in the earliest months of life but are cultivated by messages which the society conveys to the growing individual.

I have shown that, used alone, Kleinian theory cannot account for the group-protective nature of representations of threat. Findings within the SIT tradition demonstrate the inter-changeability of self and in-group protection. However, cultural theory must be drawn upon in order to encapsulate the way in which socio-historical processes enter into the contents of representations. When thinking about crises certain and not other representations are acceptable to individuals and to members of their in-group. In addition, certain groups have provided repositories for in-group projections throughout history. The way in which this comes to be known by the individual who must represent the crisis has not been explored in this chapter. The transmission of knowledge between the social environment and the individual will be explored in chapter 6.

The transposition of a model from the clinical to the social scientific setting

The unconscious and social processes posited above are difficult to observe directly. Yet the explanatory power which clinically derived concepts, such as splitting and projection, can have is evident when thinking about the empirically derived data on the plethora of risk presented in this book. Clinically derived concepts provide explanations for what, otherwise, would remain puzzling phenomena: why people imagine that they are invulnerable to disasters and link others to the source and danger of the threat.

I have suggested that it is possible to use clinically derived, psycho-dynamic concepts in the social scientific study of risk. Yet this raises certain problems. A major issue pertains to the capacity that social scientific methods have to access emotive and defensive material. Much of the psycho-dynamic theory to which I refer has been devised on the basis of observational studies and sessions with individual patients that facilitate the discharge of emotive and unconscious material in a containing environment. Mechanisms such as introjection, projection and projective identification have been inferred from the clinician's experience of the transference and counter-transference in a series of therapeutic sessions. However, the social scientific research situation contains neither an ongoing and deep-seated researcher–respondent relationship, nor the intention to contain the respondent's emotions. This raises various ethical issues. Primarily, the research may harm the respondent, if it succeeds in bringing to the surface areas of thinking which had previously been unconscious, and which had protected the respondent from anxiety. However, it must be borne in mind that defensive structures are generally robust, and the interviewer is more likely to be able to track the pathways of this defensiveness, than to elicit the anxiety itself. This was certainly the case in my study of AIDS. The space of the self and the in-group was, generally, one of purity and invulnerability. The presence of pathways of defensiveness in interview talk is corroborated by Hollway and Jefferson's (1997) study of people talking about crime.

The utility of a framework which contains psycho-dynamic concepts is that it can track traces of defences that live on in adult accounts of the events that threaten them. Psycho-dynamic thinking can step in where other disciplines flounder: it can help to look at the defences behind which societies hide what they want to forget (Green, 1995). The work of Freud and his followers has allowed for theorisation of the range of blind spots that people have. Freud initiated a tradition concerned with how and why people create and sustain their blind spots. The 'how' is accomplished by way of defences, the 'why' relates to protection against dangers which had been experienced in the individual's early life and have been reinvoked by the threat which is currently salient.

The recent work on method by Hollway and Jefferson (1997) elucidates, in practical terms, how researchers utilise clinically derived concepts in a social scientific setting. They developed a quasi-clinical interview method which aims to be theoretically driven, rather than to take respondents' accounts at face value. Their approach is guided by a primarily Kleinian notion that anxiety is a part of the human condition and that we can expect unconscious defences against this anxiety to lie at the core of subjectivity. Their method probes people's stories of the phenomenon under investigation – responses to crime – by using absences and avoidances, as much as what is said, to identify areas that are important for their respondents. They do not expect that respondents, necessarily, will be able to understand their own actions, motivations and feelings. Such understandings may lie in the unconscious, and researchers need to draw on a theory of the unconscious to discern them. A key assumption in their work is that since anxiety is a fundamental characteristic of being human, emotional concerns set up pathways for defence of the self. These pathways reveal themselves in an unstructured interview. By conducting an interview in which researchers allow respondents to give their own structure to the material, respondents provide a narrative which is created by way of unconscious associations rather than conscious logic. Pathways of thinking are also set up by emotional rather than rational motivations.

This inferential, theory-driven derivation of the effects of anxiety on defensive pathways is an unfamiliar method within the Anglo-Saxon scientific tradition where emphasis is on believing only that which is amenable to sensory validation. Mainstream psychology lacks a framework for analysing perceptions that lie outside of awareness. The energy that is dedicated to the study of the unconscious is generally channelled into 'proving' that it exists, with little attention to how it works (LeDoux, 1998). This is one reason for the jarring nature of the psycho-dynamic approach, in relation to more positivist forms of analysing responses to crises. The psycho-dynamic approach views itself as a science of the unconscious, a knowledge system of the unknown. Yet the unknown, by its very nature, is difficult to pin down and predict. Calls for methods to tap the unconscious have gained impetus in mainstream psychology in the 1990s. Lazarus (1991: 365), for example, states that 'although it is a daunting task, I believe we must . . . find effective ways of exploring what lies below the surface, how it relates to what is in awareness, and how it influences the entire emotion process.' While this call is welcome, it assumes that existing psycho-dynamic methods are ineffective.

Psychanalysis is threatening in the current Western climate in that it recognises that we are beings who at one stage had no knowledge (Phillips, 1995). It is within this very state that many of the individual's ongoing, adult responses are forged. It is a state in which 'gut level', emotively driven responses dominate. This is a truly challenging point for many aspects of contemporary psychology too, with its assumption that the individual is a self-regulating, rational information-processor rather than an essentially emotive being whose motivations are neither wholly rational nor easily fathomable. For Freud, to be a person is to be a stranger unto oneself (Kristeva, 1991; Phillips, 1995). Everything that seems bizarre has been deemed too close for comfort, and is therefore associated with the alien as a form of protection. Self-estrangement protects us from an affinity with that which has a threatening quality. That which we experience as uncanny can be traced back to something that was once familiar, but has been repressed in line with the need to become more rational and controlled. Psychoanalysis, as it stands, offers insight into the unknown. A theoretically driven interpretation of interview data, from this standpoint, offers a useful method for the analysis of unconscious material.

Psychoanalysis explores human subjective experience. This experience is so difficult to tap via positivist methods since they set up a system in which the researcher trusts only those aspects of experience that are amenable to clear-cut measurement. However, it is not just the more positivist realms of the study of humans which bypass such experience. Henriques *et al.* (1984/1998) point out that forms of narrative and discursive theory also leave out subjective experience. Discursive theory, in particular, stresses the importance of text and the meanings it creates. It does not tend to be concerned with the motivations, intentions and cognitions of those who produce or are on the receiving end of this text. An approach which overlooks subjectivity fails to explain why people repeatedly position themselves within a particular set of discourses, making their actions predictable to both themselves and to others. It also fails to account for the experience of identity, and the continuity of a sense of 'self'. People's wishes and desires, which they hold to be a part of this 'self', are obfuscated. Discursive views of the human can be as problematic as the machine-like perspective contained within the information processing models of thinking (see chapter 4).

My approach represents an antidote to highly discursive and to information processing accounts. I need to reiterate that my concern is with a subjective experience which is a sedimentation of the 'we' in the 'I'. Subjectivity is not intra-subjectively constituted. The early social environment of the child, in which needs are, or fail to be, responded to, forms the seeds of the psyche: 'These [seeds] are sedimented in affectively toned representations of self-in-relation-to-others' (Sloan, 1996: 111). Vestiges of the early, infantile representations inform later responses to ideas which are encountered in the social environment.

My approach to theorisation of the workings of human responses can be accused of methodological individualism: explaining group-rooted representations by reference to the representations of the individuals within them, a constant rerouting of responses which are linked to group membership back to the individual's psyche. I would challenge the notion that focusing on the psyche of the individual is an individualist enterprise. Although entities encased in a single, continuous skin are called 'individuals', their individuality is socially constructed. However, I find it crucial to refer to individuals as the basic units who generate responses to risks. Even a 'group' that acts in a paranoid-schizoid way does so as a result of the collective action of its individual members. Essentially, I reject a notion of a 'group mind'. This position is compatible with that of Klein and her followers, and with many who work within the social representations tradition (see chapter 6).

In the preceding discussion I have moved between the work of Klein and that of Freud as if their tenets are compatible. Although Klein's work certainly adheres to many of the assumptions of her predecessor, her ideas differs in certain aspects crucial to a theory of response to risks. The object relations departure in psychoanalysis, initiated by Klein, means that relations with objects, rather than the expression of instincts, are the basic preoccupation in the theory and in clinical work (Young, 1996). Love, hate, unconscious phantasies, anxieties and defences overshadow the earlier concern with sex, sexuality and sexual energy. Rather than the Freudian focus on psychic structures, the emphasis in the Kleinian model is on feeling states and the positions that develop around these. The spotlight on the sedimentation of the 'we' in the 'I' reflects a major transition from the Freudian stance in which the focus is on drives, and the object of drives is merely contingent upon them. Kleinian theory and related developments are highly social in relation to Freudian drive-based theory.

Even though the psychoanalytic perspective which I have presented is primarily Kleinian, it is intertwined with a key Freudian concept. Freud's life instinct is crucial in my framework since it underpins the assumption that people strive to protect a positive inner space by way of various mental operations. It is difficult to theorise the protection of a positive inner (and in-group) space other than in relation to drives. Without the concept of a 'life force' it is difficult to understand the protection of the self implied in the blaming of others at times of crisis, which is found across so many societies of both the past and the present, in relation to a plethora of risks.

A number of theorists certainly view the Freudian focus on drives and Kleinian focus on object relations as incompatible positions. This is accentuated by the simplification of Klein's work which views her as a theorist who focuses on the destructive nature of the psyche, in absolute contrast to the life force. It is also exacerbated by claims that her work is a-cultural. Green (1995) points to the impossibility, for him, of imagining Klein writing a book like Freud's culturally orientated *Totem and taboo*. Aspects of Freud's thinking spawned a number of works such as Adorno *et al.*'s (1950) classic study of prejudice, and much work within the Frankfurt school, which linked psycho-dynamic and socio-historical forces. Though Klein wrote nothing which approximated Freud's more socio-cultural writings, her progeny do just this. Many of the contemporary theorists to whom I refer in this chapter find Klein's work to be highly compatible with social theory.[5] Green (1995) makes no allusion to the whole contemporary British tradition upon which I draw, which applauds Klein for placing a relational element (between infant and primary object) at the root of psychic development, making her theory amenable to integration with social theory.

Concluding remarks

The first part of my framework for explaining the human response to potential crisis has been forged in this chapter. Its foundations lie in the human unconscious response to anxiety. Contrary to the charge that psycho-dynamic theories focus on intra-subjective experience, I showed that a highly social framework can be derived from this orientation. In this chapter I have drawn together the more clinical and the more culturally based psycho-dynamic traditions, showing that their findings are highly complementary. The combination of the two traditions provides the seeds of an explanation for why people locate threat with 'the other'. Not only does the desire to protect the self become generalised to one's in-groups, but also the anxieties that one seeks to externalise are socio-culturally shaped.

The Kleinian model is remarkably useful in terms of setting up a framework for understanding how meaning is made of threats. It locates the origin of the tendency to represent others in polarised terms, as either all 'good' or all 'bad'. Others are all 'bad' at times of raised anxiety, when paranoid feelings are projected outside of the self as a form of self-protection. However, the need to protect the self is a function of the life force, identified by Freud. Traces of the split, early responses to anxiety remain with people throughout their lives and are reinvoked when they feel threatened. The resonance of the splitting defence is so powerful because of the extreme state of dependency and helplessness in which the infant finds itself in the early months of life when it builds the defence. The mental operations which come into being at such times are shaped within a relationship with the primary object. Later in life, they are shaped by interactions with those ideas which are acceptable to the groups with which individuals affiliate. This acceptability is configured by the dominant ideas in a society.

The particular characteristic of the early, split state of being is that contradictory feelings cannot sit together. Were they to do so, this would constitute a rather complex orientation towards the crisis and towards other groups. I delve into the second of Klein's positions, the depressive position, in the final chapter of the book. It is in this position that reconciliation between the split parts is forged. This position, often neglected in socio-culturally orientated psycho-dynamic theories, lends hope that splitting is neither inevitable nor unchangeable. The effect of reconciling 'good' and 'bad' within the same object is explored. This has major implications for attempts to reduce the level of blame which arises when people are initially faced with risks.

In this chapter I have focused on the way in which anxiety impacts upon the structure of people's representations of risks. The emotional focus, and the focus on unconscious defensiveness, distinguishes my framework from the mainstream psychological frameworks. A further mark of difference lies in the status afforded to people's cultural environment in my approach. Chapter 6 pursues the links set up in this chapter, establishing how socio-historically forged ideas enter into the thinking processes of each individual. It provides an alternative social psychological framework for investigation into the 'not me' response, from that offered by the cognitive tradition.

NOTES

1 Object relations theory is a British-based development of classical Freudian theory.
2 Klein generally uses the term 'self' interchangeably with 'ego', and in Kleinian theory the ego exists from birth (Hinshelwood, 1989a). I adhere to this definition.
3 I refer to the mother rather than the 'primary object' even though the infant's 'primary object' may be a figure other than the mother. In psychoanalytic work the term 'object' refers to both the person or thing that is of interest to self in satisfying a desire (Hinshelwood, 1989a).
4 There is a debate concerning whether projection and projective identification are different processes. Meissner (1989) and Moses (1989) argue that the latter concept is not necessary since all projection involves identification. There is a further polemic concerning whether projective identification precedes projection or not, and whether projective identification is less widespread than projection (see Sandler (1989) for an exploration of the use of the concept).
5 Alford (1989) has developed a conceptualisation of what the Frankfurt theories would have looked like had they used Klein rather than Freud.

6   Social representations of risks

The second part of my framework for explaining the 'not me – others' phenomenon is presented in this chapter. A social representational rubric is chosen because it is able, epistemologically, to incorporate the socio-cultural and psycho-dynamic layers of the response to crises. In addition, it is centrally concerned with how individuals represent their worlds. It allows for exploration of how group, cultural and societal forces become sedimented in the psyche of the individual. Although the approach which I propose extends existing social representations theory, the theory already contains a highly valuable set of concepts pertaining to risks. They are explored and broadened in this chapter.

In her book about Picasso, Gilot (1965) states that painting is a mediator between the strange, hostile world and ourselves. It is a way of seizing power over the universe, by giving form to our terrors and desires. She draws an analogy between painting and the African mask. Both play a role in mediating between people and the hostile forces which surround them. Social representations play a similar role in contemporary Western societies. Humankind has a dread of powers that it cannot subdue and compensates for this impotence imaginatively, representing that which is encountered in a comforting way. What are the workings of the comforting representations of threatening social objects?

What are social representations?

The field of social representations is concerned with the explanations that people give for phenomena which they encounter in the social world. The objective of the approach is the systematic study of common-sense thinking. The originator of the theory, the French social psychologist Moscovici, states its purpose: 'These are the questions then to which we hope to find answers: What goes on in people's minds when they are faced with life's great enigmas such as illness . . . ? How do the systems of social representations . . . come into being and then evolve?' (Moscovici, 1984a: 941). A concern with how individuals arrive at common representations of phenomena, such as risks, lies at the heart of the theory. People's commentary on the world, the spontaneous philosophies they concoct in cafés, offices, hospitals and laboratories, is presumed to build up their sense of reality. The chatter that surrounds people – in newspapers and on the television, in the snippets of conversation overheard on the bus – acts like a material force. It is just as 'real' an environment to people, and as influential on the course of their actions, as more physical entities: 'where reality is concerned, these representations are all we have, that to which our perceptual, as well as our cognitive, systems are adjusted' (Moscovici, 1984b: 5).

Social representations are studied in themselves, but are presumed to underpin both thoughts and actions. Attributions of blame (see chapter 4), for example, would be underpinned by a deeper, under-lying social representation, such as that individuals engineer the consequences which befall them. This social representation allows misfortunes to be viewed as self-procured. Social representations are deep-seated; attributional and optimistic 'errors' are built upon these deeper representational structures. The link between social representa-tions and action can be demonstrated by way of empirical examples. Having reviewed the French literature on sexuality in the context of the HIV/AIDS epidemic, Giami and Schiltz (1996) show that a particular social representation underpins unsafe sexual practices in all of the studies. When people hold a representation that a partner is a 'good' one, they *do not* practise safer sex consistently. The 'good' partner includes one that is loved, long term, known, from the same social network and/or has a pleasant appearance. People are likely not to have sex or to practise safer sex with those who are represented as 'bad'. This is corroborated by Bajos *et al.* (1997) who show that condom use is inversely related to the degree of perceived intimacy, regardless of what is known about the partner's HIV status. In particular, people who represent themselves to be 'in love' are less likely to protect themselves against HIV infection. This finding has been corroborated by many studies conducted both within and outside of the social representations framework (see Joffe, 1997a).

'Social representation' refers to two notions that are interlinked. It refers to the content of understandings of the everyday world: the ideas that circulate in a society, and constitute common sense. In this sense it is similar to the lay theory, lay belief or common-sense idea. Beyond the concern with what people think, it focuses on the specific processes by which these contents are shaped.

Processes involved in social representation formation

Three key processes forge a social representation: the transformation of expert ideas, via modes of communication, into lay thinking; the imposition of past ideas on the new event that needs to be understood; and the saturation of the new event which requires interpretation with the symbolic meanings that exist in the culture. Each of these three processes will be explored in turn. The emphasis is upon how an array of forces impact on the individual's thoughts about a given event, such as a particular risk. Broadly speaking, history, culture and societal institutions, such as science and the mass media, play a major role in shaping individual representations.

For Moscovici (1984b) the transformation of scientific knowledge tends to be deemed a fundamental aspect of common sense: common sense is science made common. The finding that scientific experts are those most likely to feed common sense is based upon Moscovici's (1961/1976) extensive study of how psychoanalytic concepts came to pervade everyday talk in France. However, this point is disputable. Duveen and Lloyd (1990) illustrate that social representations of phenomena such as intelligence do not originate in the sciences. Even Moscovici's own position is equivocal. Moscovici (1984a) states that every representation is rooted either in science or in another representation. For the purpose of the discussion of social representations of mass risks, however, knowledge about them, at least in contemporary Western culture, tends to originate in the sciences. The prime position of science in this process relates to its elevated status in contemporary Western culture.

A particular concern within social representations theory is with the *transformation* that occurs as knowledge gets communicated from the more reified, scientific universe to lay thinkers. The mass media play a leading role in transforming expert knowledge into lay knowledge. The lay person's first contact with a potential crisis is often via the news media, or via other people relaying items presented in the news. The news media do not merely present a 'photocopy' of expert knowledge for lay people to assimilate. The news media have to hold the attention of mass audiences. To do so they not only simplify expert issues, but also introduce exciting angles. To this end the quarrels that occur between the experts who attempt to explain the new event are presented, as are issues of responsibility and blame. In their analysis of the news media, Brown *et al.* (1996) show that health risks are framed in a manner more related to moral outrage than to scientific notions of calculable risk. This finding, which corroborates that of Herzlich and

Pierret (1989), highlights the role of the media in a particular type of transformation process. The transformation involves the saturation of expert knowledge with the core values and social norms of the culture.

Transformation, by its very definition, involves making changes to the initial content. Moscovici (1984a) utilises this concept precisely to emphasise the modifications that occur as scientific knowledge gets represented in the mass media and then in lay terms. Even though the mass media may give issues a particular slant, it should not be assumed that the audience adopts this leaning, as if by way of direct transmission. Ideas which pervade the mass media may be accepted directly, yet their meaning may be negotiated or even challenged by lay thinkers (Hall, 1980). A particular outcome of the circulation of knowledge between science, the mass media and lay thinking is that scientific knowledge tends to acquire a moral dimension (Moscovici, 1984a). It is integrated into a moral system which regulates what is to be regarded as acceptable or unacceptable in a society.[1]

This raises a further issue: is scientific thinking free of the value dimension with which the mass media are said to inject science? Moscovici (1984b) and a number of his followers claim that scientific thinking proceeds from premise to conclusion relying upon a system of logic and proof. It utilises laws such as maintaining distance from the object, repetition of experiments, falsification and confronting evidence with counter-evidence. It epitomises the very attempt to overcome the tendency found in lay thinking, to confirm the familiar, to prove what is already known. Other researchers who utilise the social representations framework have found that the processes that occur in scientific circles, at least at the point of assimilation of new, threatening phenomena, are similar to those that occur in the media and lay realms. Herzlich and Pierret (1987) show that, while medical debates are rooted in sophisticated epidemiological models, they draw upon the 'us' versus 'them' modes of thought that exist in the society at large. My empirical work (see chapter 3) demonstrates that in the early stages of the discovery of what was later termed AIDS, many prestigious, medical and scientific papers posited links between the syndrome and 'the other': foreigners, out-groups and aberrant practices. Outside of the discipline of psychology, a body of empirical studies (e.g. Latour and Woolgar, 1979) has shown that scientific 'facts' are produced in a manner akin to the production of knowledge in other spheres. Latour and Woolgar (1979) demonstrate that solving something previously mysterious in the scientific realm is the outcome of a complex debate, in which social factors are highly visible. Yet the 'fact' which this process produces bears no trace of its social construction.

It is at points where new links are being forged, such as between nuclear fall-out and certain diseases, that there is a tension between what the experts and lay people know. This is often a time when the experts try to feed knowledge of how to avert the disaster to lay people. However, even when knowledge is not actively disseminated, lay people seek out explanations. A lack of understanding perturbs people and motivates this exploration. For Moscovici (1984b: 24) 'the purpose of all representations is to make the unfamiliar, or unfamiliarity itself, familiar'. Following from this, a key focus of the theory is the way in which *new* ideas and events are integrated by individuals. This explains why AIDS was a major focus within the social representations rubric in the 1980s and 1990s. Risks associated with genetic engineering are increasingly being studied, as we move towards the millennium. New information, at some level, is inherently threatening since it jeopardises the individual's sense of mastery of a known universe. In ancient contexts words for 'new' contained inherently negative connotations such as 'strange', 'startling' and 'unwelcome'. Yet that which is new is also associated with novelty and excitement. Notwithstanding the dual sets of emotions which can be evoked by new events, the potential risk, by definition, contains at least some degree of threat.

It is not surprising that the processes at work in early scientific, journalistic and lay thinking are similar, since the individuals who work in these spheres all begin their thinking by way of conjectures. Thereafter, they proceed along different pathways with only the scientists adopting, at least to some degree, the methods of verification mentioned above. Two specific processes are used when people, be they scientists, journalists or lay people, initially integrate new ideas: anchoring and objectification (Moscovici, 1984b). These processes ensure that the core values and norms of the society get stamped onto new events. They enable the person to forge ideas about new events in a way that induces comfort by maintaining the existing sense of order.

The link that was made initially in scientific, media and lay circles, between AIDS and 'the other', is best understood by way of the '*anchoring*' (Moscovici, 1984b) mechanism. When a new event must be understood, its integration is accomplished by taking the event which is, by definition, unfamiliar, and moulding it in such a way that it appears continuous with existing ideas. AIDS was configured in terms of past epidemics which had been linked to foreigners, out-groups and perverse practices (see chapter 2). Anchoring is not an individual process of assimilation. Rather, the ideas, images and language shared by group members steer the direction in which members come to terms with the unfamiliar. The anchoring process is a social form of the more cognitive categorisation process. This act of classification, of naming, makes the alien, threatening event imaginable and representable. Since the new phenomenon gains the characteristics of the category to which it appears similar, opinions which were held in relation to the earlier phenomenon are transferred to the new one. The classic example of this process derives from Moscovici's (1961/1976) study in which he found that people transposed the unfamiliar phenomenon psychoanalysis, to the more known concept of the Catholic confession. This removes the mysterious edge from the new phenomenon: psychoanalysis is no more than a form of confession. Of course it removes from the field of thought that which is specific and different about the new event.

The anchoring process does not explain why a particular phenomenon originally got connoted in a specific way. Why was the epidemic linked with 'the other' initially? I hope to have explained this by utilising psychodynamic concepts. What the anchoring concept does is to show how ideas get perpetuated, once they are in circulation.

In social representation formation the process termed 'objectification' works in tandem with 'anchoring', transforming the abstract links to past ideas which anchoring sets up, into concrete mental content. Unfamiliar ideas can be made familiar by being linked either to historically familiar episodes or to the culturally familiar. Objectification saturates an unfamiliar event with something more easy to grasp. A recent study of social representations of health and illness in the Chinese community in Britain (Jovchelovitch and Gervais, 1999) indicates that food objectifies a number of the more abstract systems of thought carried in this culture. Balance and harmony are considered to be basic components of health in the Chinese community, in line with the Ying-Yang principles. Manipulation of nutrition, to this end, is the first recourse to maintaining good health and preventing or curing illness. The authors conclude that food is a major carrier of social representations of health in this community. When food is prepared and eaten, traditional knowledge about health is transmitted. Objectification saturates an unfamiliar object with something more easy to grasp. For example, the concept of God is saturated with the image of the father, and it immediately becomes imaginable (Moscovici, 1984b). The trove of familiarity which is drawn upon to make a new phenomenon more concrete lies in the culture's images, symbols and metaphors (Wagner et al., 1995).

The process of objectification overlaps significantly with that of symbolisation. A fundamental function of a symbol is to provide people with a means to experience abstract content. Symbols allow people to feel that they understand a complicated scenario at just a brief glance. Ideals, values, norms, desires as well as entities such as gods and spirits are not

easy to perceive. Once symbolisation occurs, both intellectual understanding and experience of the content follows: 'symbols contain
complex messages which are being represented in a simple and vivid way'
(Verkuyten, 1995: 274). Symbols are related to an emotional charge,
rather than purely to thinking and cognitive processes. They help to
create and to maintain certain sentiments. In a social representational
study conducted during the 1991 Gulf crisis, a sample of Europeans was
asked to rate the effects of the Gulf War by choosing from a number of
images. Pictures of birds in oil consistently had the greatest impact on the
respondents, and resonated most powerfully with the crisis. When asked
why those particular images corresponded with the crisis, respondents
talked of the suffering of the innocent, of the devastating effects of war
and of defencelessness. The 'bird in oil' symbol for the Gulf crisis
expresses, among other things, sympathy with the plight of civilians
caught up in a situation which was not of their own making.

Verkuyten (1995) notes the lack of focus on symbols within psychology and sociology, as opposed to it being a focal concept within
anthropology, in which cultural symbols are held to be keys to understanding society. The concern with symbols highlights a crucial difference between the social representational approach and both purely
cognitive or purely discursive frameworks. This focus locates social
representations beyond the linguistic expressions of individual respondents. Social representations of epidemics, for example, lie in both non-
verbal symbols – 'wordless thought' (Verkuyten, 1995) – and in words.
The messages, condensed and made vivid by the pink and red ribbons
sported by many lapels worldwide, are a testimony to this. Symbols
permit people to communicate and to experience a realm beyond the
bounds of speech. Meaning is understood without verbal interaction.

I have shown that anchoring and objectification are used as tools to
integrate unfamiliar events in a manner that calms the person faced with
the crisis. The integration of new ideas in a non-disturbing fashion is
accomplished by taking the unfamiliar event and moulding it in such a
way that it appears continuous with existing ideas. The stock of familiar
representations is drawn from the collective memories that exist in
groups, as well as from existing symbols. I move on to explore why this
occurs.

What motivates the formation of particular social representations?

Having postulated that specific historical events and contemporary
symbols shape the way in which each crisis is understood, it is
necessary to decipher why certain, and not other, past events and

current symbols are chosen. The motivation to form particular representations receives considerable emphasis in the social representational field. A core motivation is identity protection, which refers, simultaneously, to the protection of in-group and self-identity. Unfamiliar events evoke unease. People's representations serve to orientate them towards gaining feelings of comfort and security. It follows that the processes involved in forming the social representation, and the end product, serve to defend individuals from a sense of personal vulnerability to the threat. Yet this defensive process is not an individualistic one. When new events are encountered individuals draw – often not consciously – on ways of thinking that have always been, and continue to be, acceptable to the groups with which they identify. When anchors are objectified, groups favour the images, symbols or metaphors compatible with in-group values. So the identity positioning of the representor determines the vision which is held of a new phenomenon. Different groups ascribe to different representations in accordance with the identities which require protection. This contributes to an explanation of why mass, incurable illnesses, among other risks, tend to get cast out onto 'the other'. This maintains the sense of comfort for the self and in-group.

At the same time as protecting self and in-group vulnerability to risks, the chosen social representation maintains the status of certain groups in a society. By imposing culturally familiar ways of thinking on each new phenomenon, social representations function to maintain the status quo in a society. The perpetuation of history and existing culture, captured in the anchors and objectifications which are used to give meaning to new phenomena, serves as a safety net for most members of a society. It makes the social world seem more familiar and manageable, but simultaneously maintains the dominance of certain groups and ideas. This function can come into conflict with identity protection function since some groups are not afforded sanctuary by dominant representations. For example, I have shown (see chapter 3) that gay men internalise dominant ideas concerning the disgusting and deviant nature of their practices and at least an aspect of their identity becomes 'spoiled', rather than protected.

A final motivation in terms of shaping a representation, is that the chosen representations foster solidarity within groups and facilitate communication between group members. Kaes (1984) indicates that shared representations provide a nucleus of identification for the group, which distinguish it from its out-groups. Linking disasters with certain 'others' builds the cohesion and identity of the in-group. Associated with 'the other' are a set of practices which, by their very 'deviance', define the norms of the society. The deviant 'other' is needed to define the upright, righteous 'self'.

Why preface representation with the term 'social'?

The social representation is a distinctive entity, differing from the more general concept of representation, lay theory or belief. Its distinctiveness stems from the very particular processes involved in its formation, and the specific functions it serves for the individual. Thus far I have not indicated why the term representation is prefaced with 'social'. There are two schools of thought concerning this issue. They are not schools in any formal sense, but their interpretations of the theory are fairly distinctive.

One strand of research sees 'social' primarily in terms of sharedness. A representation can be construed as social only if it is shared by large numbers of group members. Within this school, much energy is devoted to how one ascertains, methodologically, which aspects of a representation are consensually shared in a given population. If one espouses this 'social representation = primarily sharedness' approach, quantitative methods which are able to discern consensuality among group members regarding a particular set of attitudes are often used (see Doise *et al.*, 1993). Aspects of the work conducted in the first school are indistinguishable from the attitude tradition of research, with its focus upon individual differences (see Rose *et al.*, 1995).

Rose *et al.* (1995) argue that while sharedness may be an aspect of the definition of the 'social' in social representation, it is not the most salient one. A representation needs to exist in more than one mind for it to be called 'social', yet this is a necessary, and not a sufficient condition, for it being named as such. Utilising this starting point, the second school places less emphasis upon devising a method to tap consensuality in a society, and concentrates on the development of a robust theory of the development of social knowledge. A basic problem with the attitude model, from the stance of the second school, is that a number of people may share a representation, and act accordingly, yet they are not necessarily consciously aware of the representation. Checklist measures are unlikely to tap this level. Furthermore, this school differs from the mainstream attitude tradition in that it views social representations as both an *environment* and as entities which exist in people's minds. As a methodological consequence, the range of messages available in the culture concerning the issue under study must be sampled simultaneous to the exploration of lay thinking. Rather than viewing lay thinkers as representatives of a democratic opinion group, whose shared constellations of thought can be mapped purely by tapping individual attitudes, the latter school highlights issues such as the genesis, circulation and transformation of knowledge in a society, as well as the workings of dominant thinking.

My own stance lies within the latter school. Its premise is that group members build up understandings of new events by way of an intricate set of representational processes. Individuals' representations take shape according to historical events, and to images, symbols and metaphors, relevant to their in-groups. Consequently, the individuals' social representations contain chunks of social thinking. By subjecting the individual's representations to systematic, depth scrutiny, one taps structures of thinking germane to the groups with which the individual identifies. Surveying representative samples of people does not afford the researcher automatic insight into the sharedness of ideas in a population. A number of people may indeed share a representation, and act accordingly, yet they are not necessarily consciously aware of the representation or of its motivating forces. Tacit knowledge and underlying feelings are held to be pivotal aspects of social representation, in the latter school. They are not always amenable to direct forms of measurement. They have to be inferred from data by way of theoretical insights.

A social representations – psycho-dynamic approach to crises

Having defined my use of the term social representation, and the processes and motivations that underpin its formation, I want to put forward my synthesised social representations – psycho-dynamic approach regarding how people respond to risks. The key link is that a social representation of a risk reflects the individual's defence of the self against unwelcome emotions. The social representation integrates new, threatening information in a way that upholds the personal equanimity of the representor.

The social representation of a risk has its seeds in early defences against anxiety. When crises are encountered, infantile responses to anxiety-provoking situations are reinvoked in the adult. When the response to anxiety forged in earlier years is sparked, it manifests in split thinking. Links to undesirable events are expelled. Cutting off one's own links to bad events, in general, relates to the life force. People attempt to maintain the purity of their selves and in-groups by linking undesirable events with others. The groups with whom the individual identifies play a part in determining which events are viewed as undesirable and to whom or what they are linked. When anchors are objectified, groups favour the images and symbols compatible with in-group values. So the identity positionings of representors, rather than merely the messages to which they are exposed, determines the vision which is held of the new crisis. The processes involved in forming the representation of the threat, and the end product, serve to defend many individuals from a sense of personal vulnerability. Following from this, the most important aspects of the response to risks do not lie in how people process the information they get, but in how they feel about and explain what filters through the lens with which they look at the risk. A key concern is with the group affiliations which exhibit themselves when people represent risks, and what is protected by way of such social representations.

Unlike cognitive theories of the workings of the initial response to threat, a social representational theory of risks dwells upon emotions. In the classical study which originated the theory, Moscovici (1961/1976) went as far as to state that social representations emerge precisely in response to danger to the collective identity of the group and that, consequently, a central purpose of representation is to defend against threat. He posited that all concepts of the world are a means of solving psychic or emotional tensions, compensations to restore inner stability. Given this early work, the role of emotion has received surprisingly little attention in contemporary social representations theory. Other than my own work (Joffe, 1996a, 1996b), the (translated) works of Kaes (1984) and Jodelet (1991) are unique, in terms of the English-language literature, in their elucidation of the issue of threat. Other social representational studies, such as that of Markova and Wilkie (1987), have highlighted the need to theorise the precise role of emotions in responses to social phenomena. This emphasis requires development (see chapter 7).

I propose that a psycho-dynamic model offers an invaluable tool for developing a theory of the emotional root of the response to threat. It complements a theory of the *process* of representation formation. It provides an explanation for the recurrence of certain *contents* in representations of threatening phenomena. Primarily, threats are associated with attributes which individuals seek to disown. Bad, dirty, perverse people are the recipients of misfortunes. The contents of the social representation of any phenomenon must be derived empirically. Yet it is remarkable that Westerners and non-Westerners alike link threats with foreigners, out-groups and alien practices.

In parallel to the concentrated effort which has been made, since the 1960s, to operationalise the processes involved in social representation formation, so a strategy for theorising their common contents needs to be developed. I have shown how potential threat, and a particular pattern of response to it, play pivotal roles in the shaping of the 'not me – others' response. Psycho-dynamic thinking provides the building blocks for a theory of the emotive and defensive basis of representational activity.

The distinctive nature of this social representations – psycho-dynamic hybrid within psychology

The hybrid of psycho-dynamic and social representations theory differs from mainstream psychological theories in three key respects: it does not hold individualist, cognitivist or rationalist assumptions about human beings. It is useful to remind ourselves that Western culture views 'the individual' in a very specific way, one which differs markedly from perspectives in other cultural contexts. This is important since it impacts upon both lay explanations and formal psychological models of risks. As Geertz (1975) put it:

the Western conception of the person as a bounded, unique, more or less integrated motivational and cognitive universe, a dynamic centre of awareness, emotion, judgement, and action organized into a distinctive whole and set contrastively both against other such wholes and against a social and natural background is, however incorrigible it may seem to us, a rather peculiar idea within the context of the world's cultures. (Geertz, 1975: 48).

Conventional psychological models of the response to risks operate from this set of individualist assumptions about humans. By way of contrast, both the social representational and the object relations, psycho-dynamic approaches insist that human thought and emotion is relational at its root. The psycho-dynamic strand emphasises the relational roots of representations – casting unwanted thoughts onto others – while the social representations paradigm shows that explanations are constructed in the 'unceasing babble', the 'permanent dialogue' that people have with each other, and that the mass media have with lay people, rather than within individual minds (Moscovici, 1984b). Consequently, human thought processes cannot be modelled as if they arise within, and lie exclusively inside, individual minds.

A key contention of this book is that human thinking is distinctive from the information processing. The very notion of the mind as an information processor lends it a machine-like quality. I have indicated (in chapter 4) that one implication of a machine-like analogy conceals that which is essentially human: the sense of being alive, with the attendant emotional states. Furthermore, it obscures the symbolic, meaning-making quality of human experience. Moscovici (1984a) states that the individualist, cognitivist, rationalist view of the human is 'a terrible simplification, not only because society is not a source of information but of meaning, but also because factuality is never at the core of the exchanges between members of society. Hence you cannot expect such a process [information processing] to reveal the depths of the human mind' (Moscovici, 1984a: 963).

As an 'anthropology of modern culture' (Moscovici, 1987: 514) the social representational approach endeavours to tap these depths. In the place of attempting to track and to understand what the cognitive tradition labels 'biases in decision making', human thoughts are studied in themselves, without reference to an ideal. It is presumed that different pockets of shared knowledge in different groups delimit what each group member sees as 'rational'. Researchers enter a community as if they were delving into the psychic life of a newly discovered group. Carrying a set of theories concerning the influences of expert knowledge and of mass communications on this group, as well as the impact of cultural symbols and historical memories, researchers listen to what the group's members have to tell them. Within the hybrid approach which I propose, the researcher also carries a set of psycho-dynamic concepts relevant to the study of human responses to danger. The outcome of the analysis is not compared to a normative yardstick, one in which people are seen to be either accurate or distorted perceivers. People's own understanding, their own 'logic' and 'rationality' are logged. Having listened to what is said about sexual partners, in the examples concerning unsafe sexual behaviour cited above, researchers were made aware that interpersonal issues, such as the sense that a partner is long term and loving, inform representations of the 'good' partner. This representation, in turn, is linked to risky sex. The cognitive, predictive models, which downplay interpersonal and emotive factors, failed to discover these pivotal links. They have not focused on *meaning*, which is crucial within both a social representational and a psycho-dynamic outlook. The theories upon which I draw centre upon implicit, symbolic processes to which individuals do not necessarily have access. Theories allow one to infer implicit meanings. Internal classificatory systems inform the way people apprehend risks without them knowing it. Information about such risks is not merely conveyed to the individual's eyeballs or ears. Rather, those ears and eyeballs are embedded in certain pre-established social representations which influence how they respond to what is heard or seen. The explanations that circulate in particular groups are understood as responses to specific situations which protect the self and the in-group, set up a sense of solidarity within the in-group and maintain the status quo of ideas in a society. These explanations must not be judged relative to 'reality' or 'fact' but should be understood as entities which reflect and shape a group's sense of identity, providing a safer vision of the world.

Considerable methodological challenges ensue when researchers shift their focus away from the conscious cognitions held by individuals. They are forced to abandon the respected experimental and survey models in their quest for ecological validity. They cannot assume that the knowledge structure which underpins the thoughts and behaviours of the individual will be easily accessible. They may lie in the dynamic unconscious or in the non-conscious, tacit assumptions. Pathways for exploration of the dynamic unconscious are addressed in chapters 5 and 8. A key solution to the problem that the cultural assumptions which influence individual thinking are not always found in the private knowledge of individuals is to triangulate (Flick, 1992). This involves exploring knowledge from various angles, in structures outside of individual minds such as the mass media or medical journals, as well as in interviews with lay people. The aim is not to validate the findings from one realm against that of another. Rather, the goal is to observe the transformations that occur when knowledge circulates between the different realms. In practical terms, this tends to involve comparing texts, related to a particular phenomenon, produced in scientific journals, the mass media and in transcribed interviews with lay thinkers (as demonstrated in chapter 3). It may also involve the combination of participant observation and interviews (see Jodelet, 1991).

The approach to the study of representations of risk which I advocate deems empirical investigation to be an essential component of research. This usually takes the form of depth interviews with people, concerning their explanations of a potential crisis, alongside a measure of an aspect or aspects of the representations that circulate in the social environment. This method is not sufficiently widespread in the existing work on socio-cultural/psycho-dynamic facets of the response to risk. The work of some of the historians and cultural theorists in this field (e.g. Gilman, 1985a, 1985b, 1988) analyse the media, art and other texts and images in order to ascertain the dynamics of responses to risks. Yet, as I have discussed in chapter 1, they bypass the detailed interplay of different group affiliations in forging responses to crises.

Without devising studies which look at different group-based representations, one obscures the specific interplay of in-group and out-group sentiments at times of crisis. Epidemics have been linked to out-groups such as Jews, gays, women and prostitutes; these links have dominated the literature and art of the past, and, in contemporary times, dominate the mass media. However, not all group members hold marginalised groups responsible. Some, particularly marginalised group members themselves, hold dominant groups responsible and this manifests in conspiracy theories (see chapter 3). In addition, marginalised groups often hold themselves responsible for the crisis. I have shown that many of the gay people in my British and South African samples linked their own identity to AIDS, rather than protecting themselves by expelling all associations to it. Dominant ideas affect the ability of some group members to uphold a positive sense of in-group and self-identity.

The way in which people think about risks is linked to identity. The very notion of social identity implies that one affiliates oneself with certain groups and that one does not associate oneself with others. Yet these connections are not held in mind in a neutral way. They are affectively toned such that one feels a bond, one feels attached to certain groups, and disaffiliated from others. Identity is the earliest expression of an emotional tie we have with another person (see Hall and Du Gay, 1996). Identity is rooted in emotional connectedness. It constitutes attachments which are not visible, but that bind one to others, at least in an imaginary sense.

The very sense of a positive identity is constructed by comparing others unfavourably to the in-group. A superior positioning is thereby assured for the in-group. Yet this process is corroded if one's in-group is a marginalised group in terms of the dominant ideas of the day. Identity processes are not micro-social, as some of the contemporary social identity literature suggests. Identity is constructed within and by a milieu of dominant ideas. The social representation of a risk to which a person ascribes hinges not only on the group affiliations of the person who espouses it. It is also linked to whether the person is from a dominant or a marginalised group. Identity – either protected or spoiled – lies at the heart of representation.

A social representations framework examines the content of the thought systems of those of different group identities, rather than just the process of identity formation. Much of the content evident in one group's set of ideas bears the mark of the ideas held within other groups: gay men's spoiled identity bears the mark of the heterosexual 'not me – others are to blame' representation of AIDS initially advocated by scientists, the mass media and lay people. Similarly, conspiracy theories of AIDS, held by many marginalised groups worldwide, bear the mark of dominant ideas. They are a rhetorical defence against blaming aspersions.

In light of the approach advocated in this chapter, one would expect that many social representations theorists have worked on methods for ascertaining implicit, symbolic material. Unfortunately, the field suffers from over-reliance on verbal data. Yet empirical methods for examining the symbolic content of thought are being developed. Tools such as word and image association tasks may yield useful results. In addition, in the social representations literature on madness, drawings and participant observation have been used effectively. The study conducted by Jodelet (1991), in particular, emphasises the importance of the workings of the response to threat which have not reached a verbal level but are nevertheless informative of action. Her participant observation, which revealed that when mentally ill lodgers stayed in host families their eating utensils and clothing were washed separately from those belonging to the hosts, indicates how a representation that cannot be put into words can be enacted in another form. Fears of some form of contagion are expressed via the keeping apart of the belongings of the lodgers through 'wordless thought'.

Concluding remarks

Having forged the building blocks of my approach in chapter 5, this chapter showed how individuals use historical, cultural and societal ideas in shaping their social representations of risks. The social representational stance is distinctive in the risk area in that it opposes the notion of the biased thinker and links risk-related thought to group identity. Instead of viewing people as distorted perceivers, a legacy that stems from a highly individualist cognitive psychology, it respects people's own understanding, their own 'logic' and 'rationality'. It follows people's pathways of thought in the belief that they reveal the meanings which people have made of an event, often not consciously. The dual focus on the group-based and internal rationality aspects of people's understandings of risks is particularly useful for preventive work targeted at the reduction of risk-taking behaviours. Certain communities or groups often fail to take up behaviours suggested by the experts, and this appears irrational in terms of the logic of the scientific and policy communities. Yet particular historical and socio-cultural forces, rather than problematic individual perceptions, may be at work in this process. Rather than judging people's explanations of risks relative to a yardstick of 'reality' or 'fact', they must be understood as entities which reflect and shape a group's sense of identity, often providing a safer vision of a phenomenon.

Social representations protect not only self and in-group identities, but also the status quo in the broader society. In light of the safety and identity protection which they provide, social representations are likely to be fairly stable over time and not easily modified. Indeed, if one takes on board Douglas' (1966, 1992) assertion that the function of explanations of risks is to forge community and group solidarity, creating a boundary between the polluting outsiders and the pure insiders, there is little hope of engineering change in people's social representations of dangerous illnesses. However, the discontinuities between past and present responses to illness indicate that group-based factors, such as the augmented voice of marginalised groups, change social representations over time. I explore the potential for change in representations of risks in the final chapter of the book. The penultimate chapter (chapter 7) which follows, delves into the possibility of boosting the emotional core of social psychological work on risk.

There is a stark contrast between the framework which I advocate and one with a similar name, within mainstream health psychology. They should not be confused with one another. A growing body of work on common-sense perceptions of health threats has arisen in what is termed the 'illness representations' model. Illness representations are very different from social representations of illness. Illness representations are common-sense perceptions and conceptions of illness including how a particular illness feels, what causes it, how long it lasts and how it can be controlled (Leventhal *et al.*, 1997). Illness representations are viewed as the mental operations of the individual problem solver. They are treated from an intra-psychic perspective, as are many other cognitive concepts. Interestingly, researchers who utilise the illness representations approach seek to understand 'how individuals arrive at common representations of diseases' (Leventhal *et al.*, 1997: 39). They also declare a need for a theory which brings social contextual factors into their model. However, it is inappropriate to treat the response to a threat from an intra-psychic angle, and then to expect to gain understanding of the social processes that underpin it. There is recognition of this problem within the illness representations literature itself. Leventhal and Nerenz (1985) state that their approach has only a partial understanding of illness representations, since it lacks a grasp of the contextual factors which impact upon them. They say of such contextual factors: 'Their study requires methods that we have not discovered' (Leventhal and Nerenz, 1985: 549). If such methods are to be discovered, a radical shift away from the cognitions held by individuals will have to take place. A more truly social psychological approach, such as the one advocated in this chapter, is called for.

NOTES

1 While I showed, in chapter 3, that scientific knowledge itself is infused with a value dimension, this does not detract from the central issue, which is that people make sense of 'information' in line with certain agendas, rather than in a manner analogous to information processing conducted in a computer-like fashion.

Emotional life: a new frontier for social
     theory

The social science of the 1990s has seen a resurgence in interest in the emotions. Despite emotion having been the concern of philosophy for many centuries, the contemporary science of emotion has tended to be produced by those working within a psychological framework. The primacy of psychology in the emotions field as a whole relates to a conceptualisation of emotion as a matter of individual expression and experience (Strongman, 1996). It is also linked to the rising legitimacy of neuro-psychological explanations in science more generally. The focus on the intra-psychic aspects of emotion has thwarted the development of theories of emotion in terms of their more social, cultural and historical attributes. However, the socio-cultural approach has recently gained ground. In this chapter I evaluate key components of the current emotions literature. I build up a conceptualisation of emotional life which is essentially relational and cultural, but not always accessible to consciousness. My concern is with the insight that the emotions literature offers into the response to risks, often mass risks. This response manifests in the representations of the risks which are formed. This chapter is less focused upon risk and 'the other' than the preceding chapters. It examines a literature which has not previously been linked with risk, but which provides interesting angles on fear and the self-protective elements which are crucial for a theory of the response to risks.

Recent psychological approaches to emotion

The ideals of rationality and free will have formed the cornerstones of Western intellectual and ethical traditions for over two thousand years (Averill, 1974/1996a). Concomitant to the valuing of such properties, emotions have been associated with qualities that are regarded as inferior. Western experts and lay people alike have viewed emotion as a quality that is natural (rather than cultural) and physical (rather than mental). In addition, emotions have been viewed as properties which represent the very antithesis of rationality, order, volition and control. It is not surprising, then, that strands of both the science of emotion (e.g. see LeDoux, 1998) and lay talk, view emotion as something that is passively experienced. People talk of being 'paralysed' by anxiety, 'gripped' by fear or 'seized' by anger (Averill, 1980). They 'fall' rather than 'climb' into love. As a corollary of these various properties, the emotions are imagined to come from that part of the soul or body that is common to humans and animals.

Biological and cognitive perspectives

Psychologists who posit continuity between the emotional faculties of all species have had a major impact on mainstream psychology. Their primary affiliations are with physiology and neurology. I shall highlight the work of LeDoux (1998) as an example of this trend. His ideas are relevant because he focuses upon fear and the organism's protection from it. He defines emotions as 'biological functions of the nervous system' (LeDoux, 1998: 12). They are linked to the biological imperative of species to protect themselves. LeDoux argues that in evolutionary terms emotional processes occurred in brains prior to conscious and verbal processing. This makes the non-conscious level, which is similar across animal and human, a more primary function of the brain. For this, as well as ethical and practical reasons, rats can be studied to understand the neural basis of emotional life across the species. LeDoux (1998: 125) claims that his work does not address 'what most people consider the most important, in fact, the defining feature of an emotion: the subjective feeling that comes with it'. Operating from his theoretical outlook, there is no need to study the conscious, feeling part of human life since feelings are the vehicles through which emotions are known to humans, but the systems underlying emotions are similar across species and are based upon biological functions. Feeling afraid, for example, is a result of becoming consciously aware that a biological system of the brain, such as a defence system, is active.

LeDoux's neo-Jamesian approach appropriates the term 'emotion', and redefines it in a much narrower sense than many would find appropriate for human psychology.[1] Human emotion is intricately connected with awareness. Humans know their sadness, joy and love through the subjective meanings that these have for them. Subjective, conscious feelings are not 'red herrings' or 'detours' in the scientific study of emotion, as LeDoux suggests. The growth in confidence in the brain sciences, as the future tools for unravelling the workings of the psyche, has both negative and positive implications for the study of emotions. It is problematic in that even if neuro-psychologists recognise the importance of subjectivity, its study is not easily amenable to their methods. However, the focus on those aspects of emotion which are non-verbal and unconscious represents an interesting turn in psychology, one which may have important repercussions for how responses to risk come to be understood.

At present, the cognitive position on emotion is dominant within psychology. Originally this approach advocated that physiological fluctuations were an essential, but not the sole, component of emotion (e.g. Schachter and Singer, 1962). Subsequently, cognitive theorists have questioned the role played by the biological level in producing emotions. They point to a lack of empirical support for the contention that a biological level of arousal must always be present for emotion to occur (Cornelius, 1996). Whether the biological level is essential or not, the cognitive strand of emotions research advocates that biologically generated elements have to be enriched by meanings before becoming emotional experience (e.g. see Leventhal, 1980). Therefore, contemporary cognitive approaches stress that emotions require thought: 'emotions are generated by judgements about the world' (Cornelius, 1996: 115). Appraisal is the cornerstone of the contemporary cognitive tradition, and this applies equally within and outside the emotions field. The optimal manner of finding out how people make appraisals is to ask them to introspect and to state both their appraisal and its antecedents. Therefore the emphasis is on the conscious, verbally accessible aspects of emotion.

How do empirically minded psychologists, increasingly interested in the emotional aspects linked to the appraisal of risks, tap 'emotion'? Work on risk from a social-cognitive perspective currently contains surprisingly little focus on emotions. Existing models are concerned with the link between risk-related attitudes and behaviours. Manstead and Parker (1996) and Manstead et al. (1995) refer to a distinction between affective and cognitive-instrumental aspects of attitudes towards risky behaviours. They point out that models such as Ajzen's widely used Theory of Planned Behaviour (TPB) emphasise the cognitive to the detriment of the affective component. Other researchers (e.g. Haddock and Zanna, 1998) have also noted this emphasis. Recently, energy has been invested in more emotive variables. Manstead and colleagues add the variable 'affective evaluations' to the standard TPB constructs in order to capture the latter type of attitude. They show, at least in relation to driving risks, that affective attitudes to behaviour are better predictors of behavioral intentions than cognitive-instrumental attitudes are.

Their emphasis upon affect is timely. Yet it raises the issue of the extent to which people have access to their affects, which include emotional responses and feelings. Affective attitudes are gleaned by way of questions which ask respondents how they feel when they conduct the risky behaviour under investigation. The issue of access to inner states reflects the more fundamental debate in psychology concerning whether answers given by people on how they think or feel should be trusted, or are unreliable.

One side of the debate holds that researchers should value the human ability to account for their emotions. This resource has been neglected by psychologists, historically (Greenwood, 1994). For the researcher who is interested in the subjective, feeling aspect of emotions, surely knowledge of the emotion is its defining feature. People know what they feel. Among those who advocate such a position, some favour more open-ended, self-reports and others predefine response categories, thereby facilitating a straightforward comparison between different people's responses. However, highly directive questions which are accompanied by predefined response categories may be particularly problematic for tapping 'affective evaluations'. They force people into response choices which do not necessarily map onto their own feelings (Haddock *et al.*, 1993).[2]

An open-ended response option to the 'what do you feel' question may allow researchers to overcome this problem. Open-ended measures allow researchers to tap idiosyncratic responses. They reflect an individual's 'stored reaction' to the phenomenon under investigation, rather than a reaction elicited by way of forced choice between predefined options. Haddock and Zanna (1998) have established that they can be both *reliable* and *valid* measures of the components of an attitude. They appear in a number of recent social-cognitive pieces of research. For example, Dijker *et al.* (1996) investigated feelings about racial groups and followed a closed-ended measure with instructions which read: 'If a certain feeling has occurred (it does not matter how seldom or how often it has happened), please try to describe the things that have caused the feeling. Write down everything that comes to mind, both small and big. Things you may find unreasonable are also important to mention' (Dijker *et al.*, 1996: 318). This form of inquiry aspires toward higher levels of ecological validity than the checklist questionnaire. Yet it still contains an inherent problem of self-reported data: that people may not have access to the causes of their emotional states, particularly their 'unreasonable' feelings.

Those who deem self-report data unreliable claim that people are often in the dark as to why they feel the way that they do (see LeDoux,

1998). Reasons people give for a feeling are not the same as the causes. People may know what they feel, but not how or why the feeling came about. The cause of an emotion often involves what LeDoux terms 'a history stored in memory' in interaction with an immediately present stimulus. Anxieties linked to an early experience of death may be evoked when faced with images of fellow group members suffering from war, for example. Yet the individual who feels highly anxious when witnessing disturbing images of in-group members may not have access to all of the sources of such feeling, when asked to comment about them.

Self-reports provide an inroad into the feelings that exist in consciousness. However, since a lot of the material which underpins emotional processing lies in the unconscious, self-reports, when used alone, cannot provide a complete picture of emotional life. From the mid-twentieth century psychologists have tried to prove, experimentally, that emotions can occur in the absence of conscious awareness. After a hiatus in this research it was reinvigorated in the 1980s by the work of Zajonc (1980), which showed that emotional reactions could be formed without conscious registration of the emotion-eliciting stimuli. For psychologists such as LeDoux these studies indicate that conscious 'introspection', which is what produces the self-report, is not a solid foundation for understanding emotions. He turns to neurological research in animals as a solution to the problems of self-reports. Experimentation on the non-conscious processing of danger in rats is used as the basis of an explanation of the human emotional system. However, whatever the advantages of the data gleaned in this way, precisely because he focuses on neurological aspects of animal emotion no light can be cast upon the subjective aspect of human emotion.

A dilemma arises. On the one hand, feeling is only feeling because of awareness: to feel something, by definition, is to have conscious awareness of a state. Feelings are the vehicles through which humans come to know their emotions. Feelings are subjective phenomena. A subjective phenomenon, by definition, exists only when it reaches the conscious level of human awareness. Even if consciousness is only the tip of the mental iceberg, as originally posited by Freud, it is an intrinsic part of what it is to feel. On the other hand, there is strong evidence for the existence of facets of emotional life which are not readily accessible from consciousness. LeDoux may well be correct in his supposition that: 'The emotional unconscious is where much of the emotional action is in the brain' (1998: 64) and that 'Emotions . . . operate in some psychic and neural space that is not readily accessed from consciousness' (1998: 71). However, the crucial point is that the tip of the iceberg and the expanse that rests beneath the tip constitute the iceberg. Emotional life is comprised of both feelings and unconscious facets. Despite the daunting nature of the task, there is a need to understand what lies below the surface *in relation to* what exists in human awareness. Neither feelings nor unconscious processes has primacy over the other. Self-reports can augment understanding of subjective aspects of emotional life, and experiments may be able to provide insight into non-cognitive aspects. However, at present, neither explains the relationship between the two. Neither is able to decipher how unconscious elements impact upon self-reported experience.

A broader view of emotion in psychology

Cornelius (1996) raises a number of simple questions which pave the way to a broader view of emotional life than those encapsulated in traditional cognitive and biological views. Why do men weep less, in the presence of others, than women do? Why is weeping variably acceptable in different cultures? Attention to gendered and cultural variations raises problems for both biologically and cognitively determined theories of emotional life. Expressing a weep is not a 'natural' function of sadness. A purely biological, essentialist focus overlooks how social constraints moderate what are construed as biologically driven functions. In relation to cognitive psychology, a focus on emotions as a function of individual appraisal neglects the interpersonal, unconscious and cultural determinants of cognitions.

One approach to studying emotion is to weight the different aspects of emotional life equally, but to attend to just one aspect. This would justify the choice between a biological, a cognitive or a more inter-subjective approach. Alternatively, Parrott and Harré (1996) propose that emotions should be studied integratively with the view that emotions are at once expressions of judgement and bodily, at once socio-cognitive and somatic. Operating from this standpoint studies of emotion, ideally, should encompass these apparently disparate elements. However, a further strand of research challenges the relevance of the biological angle in the study of all emotions. Social constructivist and existential lines of thinking indicate that it is not appropriate, in terms of certain emotions, to include a biological element. Averill (1974/1996a), for example, contends that it is possible to have an emotion in the absence of physiological correlates, a line of thinking that certainly contradicts contemporary neuro-psychological findings. Only the most studied emotions, namely fear, arousal and anger have such correlates. Hope, envy and gratitude do not. Too close an association between emotion and physiological activity has been achieved by overlooking contrary, and equally compelling evidence. According to Averill, even though some emotions have their roots in human biology, and have been evolutionarily necessary (e.g. avoidance of certain dangers), 'most standard emotional reactions transcend any biological imperatives related to self or species preservation' (Averill, 1974/1996a: 223). According to Averill, if investigations of emotion are broadened into emotions such as hope, envy and gratitude, dominant theories of emotion will be forced to change substantially.

The biological link is also put into question by the limited nature of the findings on biological structure: the amygdala is involved in reactions of animals that humans label 'fear', but few other regions of the brain have been directly linked to emotional states. A further factor which undermines the biologically based theories is that despite the biological similarities in human brains, there are individual differences concerning emotional states and reactions (Ginsburg and Harrington, 1996).

The argument against the reduction of emotion to a series of physiological responses can be developed by using existential, social constructionist and psycho-dynamic strands of reasoning. The existential position's *raison d'être* is to explore precisely why emotion cannot be reduced to a series of physiological responses. Crossley (1998) states that while emotions involve physiological reactions, they are not reducible to them. He points out that a single bodily response, such as crying, can be related to joy, sadness or fear. Therefore this physiological act does not indicate the specific identity of the emotion. The experiential level of emotion, which is not reducible to any other more 'basic' aspects, must form a focus in its own right. The psychology of human beings must focus on the quality that sets them apart from animals: consciousness. Awareness of feelings is intrinsic to human emotional life.

Emotions are constituted not only by experiential states, but also by group norms. Greenwood's (1994) social constructionist model hinges upon the premise that other people and their norms teach people which emotions are appropriate in particular situations. This instils representations within individuals concerning the appropriateness of the emotions. Children learn to be ashamed of their epileptic attacks when they come to represent and to treat the behaviour related to the attack as humiliating. Feeling this emotion is contingent upon buying into the conventions which exist in the social environment. Greenwood extends his theory across the broad terrain of emotion, and mentions envy, anger, pride, disappointment, remorse and jealousy. While his theory is valuable in highlighting how social factors, and representations of such factors, actually play a role in forging emotions, it is undermined by his choice of the most socialised, conventionalised emotions to talk of emotion as a whole. He bypasses important emotions, such as love, hate and fear which may contain less normative elements. The latter set of emotions are particularly important in a theory of response to risks.

Psycho-dynamic strands of theorisation centre upon love, hate and anxiety and situate inter-subjective, though not (generally) group normative, elements at the source of the development of emotional life. Emotional life is moderated by relationships rather than being a predetermined aspect of human beings. The genesis of emotional life springs from the emotions that accompany the affective bond between infant and primary caregiver. Bowlby's (1969, 1973) classic work, firmly corroborated in recent years (Fonagy *et al.*, 1993; Benoit and Parker, 1994), demonstrates that the quality of the early relationship forms a prototype for later social relations. Within their earliest relationship with the primary caregiver, infants evaluate the signals that they get. The outcome of this evaluation is a subjective experience of either security or insecurity. A non-empathic early caregiver who gives love inconsistently creates an internal representation or model for the individual's subsequent relationships, an untrusting, insecure model of self-with-other. On the other hand, an empathic caregiver can provide a secure, inter-subjective model for the individual.

The Bowlby model highlights emotions such as love and trust. It provides a basis for understanding differing levels of trust within groups, based upon individual biographies. The Kleinian and neo-Kleinian strands of theory (see chapter 5 for exposition of this model), on the other hand, hinge upon responses to early states of anxiety. Klein's model is highly analogous to Bowlby's in positing that emotionally underpinned representations are forged in the relationship between primary caregiver and infant. Aspects of the infant's experience of this interaction become internalised, establishing representations which inform how people's emotions operate throughout their lives. In such representations, self becomes associated with positive feelings and others with the unwanted parts of experience.[3] The contents of these representational structures develop in line with the social representations which are held dear in the groups with which people affiliate and attach themselves in the course of their lives. The social environment lends ideas concerning what it is to be 'good', rather than 'bad', in the particular culture.

Aspects of the existential position are highly complementary to the psycho-dynamic strands of thought advocated by both Bowlby and Klein. Merleau-Ponty (1962) indicates that individuals' emotional spheres are produced in relationships. Repeated emotional responses become sedimented in the individual over time, forming a particular emotional repertoire for that individual. Emotional responses will point backwards, to the person's history of relationships. As in psychoanalytic thinking, this emotional repertoire is regarded as fairly stable and so each person's emotional ways of being are relatively permanent. Of course this approach allows for the notion of events acting to constrain or to exacerbate certain emotions, and defence against becoming overwhelmed by them.

Baring in mind the inability of current psychological methods to decipher the connection between feelings and non-conscious processes, do more appropriate methods exist? The case study of AIDS (presented in chapter 3) demonstrates that a theoretically driven analysis of semi-structured interviews, in concert with thematic analysis of scientific and media output, yields a link between what is said and forces beneath the surface of consciousness. Self-reports are a key access point to representations of emotions and their outcomes in the representational process. However, since people are not always aware of the sources of the ideas and affects upon which researchers ask them to reflect, theory is used to understand the data. The roots of cognitively accessible facets of emotional life may lie in the cognitive unconscious,[4] the dynamic unconscious or in the tacit assumptions of the culture. The dynamic unconscious, in particular, is structured on the basis of emotional roots. A psycho-dynamically driven analysis of the meaning of self-reported information – which explores a range of possible connotations – can greatly enhance understanding of the facet of emotional life under investigation. Theory allows one to make the leap from what is said by respondents to material that is not explicitly present, but nevertheless underpins their responses. One can rely on verbal and written data, but make inferences, rather than rely on a purely empirically driven observation of what is said. The recognition that what research participants reveal to researchers does not necessarily communicate what emotional states make them act and think in the way that they do, may lead to the development of new methodologies which provide access to untapped areas.[5]

My concern is with how risks, often mass risks, are experienced by adults. Using a diary method, Oatley (1998) shows that 20 per cent of human emotional incidents are not related to immediate events but are elicited at one remove: by memories, by imagination, or by symbolic means such as reading or watching visual images. Such emotions are elicited by representations. This is particularly important in that it shows that human emotional life is not constituted purely by responses to immediate stimuli. Responses to fear, in the direct sense found in rat studies, bears little relation to these once removed emotions. Animal studies offer little insight into the evocation of emotion via representation. However, it is interesting to note that the self-protective function of the human response to risk, identified in my social psychological approach, bears similarity to the more socio-biological stance concerning the impetus to guard against danger due to self and species preservation. I have argued that it is useful to view emotion, and the defence against overwhelming emotions, as part of the individual's representational field, one which frequently guards the individual from a sense of fragmentation, protects identity and also maintains the status quo at a more societal level. Even social constructionist thinkers such as Averill, who eschew the links between most emotions and evolutionary imperatives, accept that responses to danger relate to self and species preservation. The universalist notion, from the evolutionary perspective, is particularly interesting because the self-protective response to risk seems to contain a universal element, though particular social forces impact upon it differentially. The idea of a life force, from Freud's work, which drives the process, is in keeping with the theory of self and species preservation.

Recent socio-cultural perspectives on emotion

Having delved into psychological approaches to emotional life, I turn to an investigation of socio-cultural perspectives. By definition, the sociological and cultural theory literatures take little heed of physiological and intra-psychic notions of emotion. They do not focus on individual expression and experience. Yet they can be used to cast light upon individual, subjective responses in particular contexts.

The exploration of emotion from a cultural perspective reveals a powerful link between emotion and control in the West. Even though, or perhaps because, in the West emotions are regarded as irrational, uncontrollable states thath befall people, the emphasis on the attempt to control them is among the most important insights that cultural studies offers. In the United States, when people talk about their emotions, a strong set of metaphors is used concerning controlling the emotions and the situations leading to them (Lutz, 1996). The way in which grief and regret have been handled in different ages illustrates this. In Victorian culture there was a preoccupation with grief, whereas in the twentieth century excessive sorrow has been frowned upon. This change is linked to the increased valuing of self-control (Stearns and Knapp, 1996). Like excessive grief, the North American worldview renders regret almost socially impermissible: there is a strong norm which emphasises positive, and downplays the negative, emotions (Landman, 1996).

Interestingly, this norm is reflected in empirical findings which link positive illusions about the self to high levels of coping and to the non-depressed demeanour. Taylor and Brown (1988) produce strong evidence that mental health rests on exaggerated perceptions of personal control and on optimistic bias. I have shown (see chapter 4) that optimism may also be linked to better physical health. However, an exaggerated sense of control is associated with a sense of invulnerability to danger, which is not always functional since it may inhibit the taking of precautions in relation to dangers. An overriding sense of invulnerability seems to be particularly strong in cultures, such as the North American one, which are orientated towards the ethos of control.

A focus on culture highlights how emotions are experienced differently cross-culturally rather than being uniform across people and species. Cross-cultural research by linguists and anthropologists challenges the tenet that there are a universal set of basic emotions,[6] a cornerstone of the mainstream psychology of emotions. Lexical research shows that concepts such as happy and angry are cultural artefacts of Anglo-culture reflected in the English language, rather than being universal. Wierzbicka (1994), for example, points out that anger does not have a direct equivalent in Polish. The closest word has different connotations. Similarly, the English notion of 'being upset' has no exact Polish equivalent. People identify their feelings in terms of concepts provided by a language and a cultural system. It is not possible to divorce different ways of talking about emotions in different languages from the differential subjective experiences. The cultural arguments which I have raised would suggest that imminent dangers, or 'risks', as modern Western cultures term them, would be couched in cultural ideas. Indeed, in Western culture concepts of control and threats to control are central to the reading of danger. For Douglas the very term 'risk', a Western concept, refers to control from future dangers via objective systems of calculation and regulation. Following from this, the subjective experience of danger in the West is likely to be orientated towards mastery of the danger. This fits well with the vast empirical and theoretical literature in the social sciences which indicates that the representations which arise at times of potential danger serve to control, to limit the representor's sense of vulnerability to, the risk.

Like cultural theory and anthropology, sociology offers considerable insight into emotional life. Owing to the valorisation of reason in the Western intellectual tradition, sociology, like psychology, has favoured the exploration of (socially based) knowledge and cognitive processes over a focus on emotions. Mestrovic goes as far as to state that: 'The missing ingredient in most sociological theorising is the role of the *emotions*' (Mestrovic, 1997: xi, original italics). For him this applies to both modernist and postmodernist theories. However, there is counter-evidence for this. I have shown (see chapter 1) that anxiety is a guiding principle in major strands of modernist sociological theorisation, most notably, Giddens' (1991) and Beck's (1986/1992) work on risk, and that trust is a major theme in Wynne's (1995) work. In addition, strong emotional themes existed in the work of the early sociologists. Marx explored the sense of alienation that resulted from certain material conditions, Durkheim the underpinnings of feelings of solidarity and Weber the anxiety inherent in the spirit of capitalism (see Hochschild, 1998). Perhaps Williams and Bendelow's (1998) position is more fitting: that a distinct corpus of work on emotion has arisen in sociology only since the late 1980s.

Some of the distinctive aspects of the contemporary sociology of emotion pick up where the fathers of sociology left off and are highly pertinent to a study of the emotions that surround risks. I have referred to Beck's and to Giddens' stance on risk. I turn to the work of Mestrovic (1997) and other sociologists. Ultimately, their contribution to the contemporary apprehension of risk must be assessed.

Despite a number of flaws, Mestrovic's work paints a fascinating picture of the social forces that impinge upon the emotional aspects of self in contemporary Western society. Mestrovic (1997) views contemporary social life as 'postemotional' and those who live in such societies, 'postemotional types'. Postemotionalism began in the United States in the 1960s. The replacement of traditional ways of eating, sometimes termed McDonaldisation, extended to standardised, rational and coldly efficient ways of conducting emotional life. This manifests in a wide array of the facets of emotional life. Where once events such as going on holiday or on a date were personally, privately and idiosyncratically arranged, they now come pre-packaged. Emotional life becomes commercialised: the pre-written Valentine or Mother's day card symbolises this.

Where once emotions were private, the people produced by postemotional society bare their most intimate secrets to the cameras in a way that previous generations could not have imagined. Public displays of intimacy are the norm and this manifests in the proliferation of television shows like the American *Oprah*. Change in emotional life is also reflected in the constant attempts that are made to manipulate people's emotions. Professional enterprises and politicians constantly manage the impressions they form, rather than expressing spontaneous emotions. A part of the 'spinning' process is to adapt the message in order to elicit the desired emotions. 'Spin' exists as a function of professionals and politicians recognising the power and reach of the mass media's angle. However, from the perspective of the consumer there is a loss of ability to be taken in by the present, to be drawn into a spontaneous state of emotion. This results not only from awareness of the manipulation inherent in spin. People are also exposed to so many mass-mediated tragedies that they have 'compassion fatigue'. At best people have feelings of sympathy for all sides, of neutrality. In general, however, these factors contribute to the fundamental disengagement that one finds at the heart of postemotional society, according to Mestrovic. Deadened disengagement relates both to an overload of tragic events and to people having become cynical because they know that events are constructed, that professionals and politicians put a particular 'spin' on events in line with what they want the public to believe.

Mestrovic's thesis casts light upon the increased intervention in emotional life by spin doctors, the mass media and commercial initiatives. However, a key difficulty with his argument is its generalised nature. All facets of emotional life appear to be absorbed into a public ambit. Postemotionalism has spilled into all emotional moments – no relationship or experience is free of disengagement. Little happens to individuals other than via the vicarious experience of tragedies, the witnessing of spin-doctored issues, as well as the odd package holiday, dating agency experience or McDonald's birthday party.

A further aspect of this generalised approach is that no distinction is made between different sets of people. People in the West are 'postemotional types'. There is no allusion to people taking up socially circulating currents differentially, in accordance with their identity positioning. The non-'happy Mac' eaters, the growing number of people who eat organic food and who are vegetarian attest to a diverse range of 'types' and identities. Their group-based beliefs position them in a wholly different realm to that of fast food. Of course one may argue that the trend towards eating organic food is just the response to the McDonaldisation of society: it merely reacts to the dominant inclination, thereby proving the hegemony of the trend towards standardised, processed food. Even if this is the case, lacking in Mestrovic's argument is reference to people being variably open and suggestible to, as well as opposing of, dominant societal and consumer forces.

The approach also fails to explore the complexity of the responses to the phenomena about which it commentates. Those who volunteer to be on the baring-the-soul programmes such as *Oprah* are a self-selected sample. The very act of choosing to go on such a programme, suggests a desire to exhibit a private array of emotions in public. This exhibitionism is not forged by internal processes alone. Of course the normative environment makes a more explicit, intimate discourse acceptable in public spaces and thereby goes some way to construct exhibitionism. However, those who would not contemplate such a display are absent from Mestrovic's vision. Perhaps only a minority of people in the 'postemotional' society enter into public displays of intimacy. When they do, the disengagement which Mestrovic attributes to such 'types' is absent. People on shows such as *Oprah* certainly exhibit a range of intimate emotions publicly, but they do so with strong displays of emotion: sobbing in sadness, shouting in anger. The fundamental disengagement of the 'postemotional type' is not in evidence either in the participants or in the audiences for whom the programmes appear to be emotionally exciting.

Despite these unresolved aspects of Mestrovic's vision, his emphasis upon the shifts that have occurred in public, emotional life, and the deadening effect that they may have on spontaneous responses, is enlightening. Theory that explores the specific influence of media-led feeling, rather than intra-psychic, biologically led emotion, is valuable for the social science of risk. Interestingly, the social representational stance contains none of the doubts concerning the assimilation of media messages expressed in Mestrovic's and in other sociological writings. I turn to further sociological work on the mass media and to the problems it raises concerning the vicarious experience of events, particularly those that are threatening.

Many of the threats which I have discussed throughout this book first confront people on their television screens. Sociologists argue that the vicarious experience of threat is very different from the direct experience of it. In a similar vein to Mestrovic (1997), Tester (1998) claims that the horrors conveyed on television have a minimal impact on their contemporary, Western viewers. For Tester (1998), a key reason for this is that the television presents a desensualised world, one denuded of touch and smell. By definition, it also removes the images it shows from their wider context, and emphasises their aesthetic over their emotional qualities. Augmenting this, Bauman (1993) points to how the characters are confined to a screen, with the implications of the reduction of their complexity to two dimensions, which lack the power to engage one emotionally. Tester (1998) draws an analogy between television culture and the vision of the metropolis advocated by Simmel (1903/1971) in which the nerves are so agitated by the plethora of stimuli that reactions are deadened. The television offers so many stimuli that people stop engaging and allow the stimuli to wash over them. Precisely because of this numbness, there is a craving for excitement and for extreme stimulation. The blasé person looks to risky situations to feel alive.

Again, while this idea of the blasé-making aspects of the media seems plausible, it overlooks an equally compelling set of experiences in order to attain its clarity and conviction. Williams (1998) argues that there is good reason to believe that there is some personal identification with the tragedies presented on television. Horrifying images can become indelibly etched upon people's minds, calling forth a range of emotions. Excitement in relation to sporting events and sexual desire in relation to erotic representations are certainly evoked by the mass media. What the media lack, be they interactive (as with the Internet) or not, is the contact with another's embodied gestures such as an affectionate hug. Even though there is undoubtably a loss at this physical level, emotion is also elicited by representation. I have mentioned empirical psychological work which shows that emotion can often be evoked at one remove, by a memory or an image. Analyses which pinpoint the deficits, at a perceptual level, of the television experience, when compared with 'real life' encounters, overlook the symbolic or meaning-making processes that are so central to human 'information processing'. Emotionally tinged memories, desires and motivations can be elicited by both 'real' and mass mediated experience.

A final point concerning the impact of mass-mediated messages on feelings about events pertains to the increasing globalisation of such messages. The globalisation of media messages has certainly informed many people of far-off tragedies and risks. People come into contact with a far greater number of risks as a result. On the one hand, this may lead to feeling of emotional overload. However, the very distance of the event from the viewer's own domain, may, in itself, engender a neutrality, a lack of attachment to the event. When watching far-flung tragedies, when images are beamed from the far corners of the earth, viewers are likely to lack identification with the events, or to identify equally with many different parties. Identification or attachment suggests a bond. Without this, why should there be compassion? Viewers may find it difficult to discern, in the terms which I have suggested (see chapter 5), who can most easily be identified with the 'good' self and who with the 'bad' other. Those vicariously experiencing the Bosnian war or Northern Irish conflict, with no attachment to any of the parties, with no identities which warranted protection, observed a tangle of interests. Identification is inherently linked to loving certain people and groups and hating others. Without it perhaps viewers are emotionally neutral or mildly sympathetic to all sides. In pre-mass-mediated times and in cultures without such technology, people confront fewer events in which they hold no personal investment. The very bringing of far-off events into masses of homes may fail to evoke strong feelings owing to a lack of attachment to that which is being shown. Compassion fatigue or other symptoms of modern living may be irrelevant.

The other side of the globalisation-of-risks coin must also be kept in mind. One of the consequences of globalisation is that many risks have the potential to transfer from place to place. The contagion inherent in certain health risks provides an obvious example of this, though various environmental and industrial risks also have knock-on effects in far-flung areas. A war in a distant place also has the potential to affect self and in-group in that it could trigger a series of reprisals which bring one's own country into the scenario. Apparent disengagement from early television pictures of people with AIDS in Africa, or from images of the Gulf War, may reflect a defensive reaction, a failure to believe that the 'bad' outside has the potential to invade the self's equanimity. This is a different state from that of being blasé. It implies a defence of the self against a threat, rather than a distant, disengaged stance which springs from indifference and neutrality. They may, of course, manifest in the same veneer of disengagement: 'not me – not my group'.

Concluding remarks

In this chapter I have brought to light a number of the newer strands in the psychological, cultural and sociological study of emotional life. These texts provide food for thought. The psychological literature points to the current dominance of cognitive theories and methods, with their focus on appraisal and self-reports of emotional states, but the ascendance of neuro-psychological theories. The latter favour examination of physiological processes over judgements as the key to insight into emotional life, and tend to utilise animal experimentation to this end. The less dominant theories in the psychology of emotion are social constructionist, existentialist and psycho-dynamic strands of thought. They offer rich pickings concerning the relational roots and ongoing social dynamics which rest at the core of emotional life. They also offer a focus on subjectivity. One can focus on behaviour and behavioural expressions in animals, since their subjectivity or representational life, if it exists, is not easily accessible. Human emotional life must be studied with reference to the human ability to reflect upon subjective feelings, since this reflection forms a major component of what humans experience as emotion. However, the unconscious aspects of emotion, to which individuals do not have access, must also be addressed since they are part and parcel of accessible emotional life.

Texts which provide students with overviews of theories of emotion (e.g. Cornelius, 1996; Strongman, 1996) do not allude, or allude negatively, to psycho-dynamic theories of emotion. Strongman's rationale for this is that 'This type of theory is not easy to understand nor is it easy to be convinced of its worth' (1996: 20). More specifically, in relation to anxiety, Strongman states: 'Psycho-analytic theories of anxiety began with Freud and have not developed a great deal since' (1996: 162). Such views are surprising when set against the thriving literature on attachment and the Kleinian and neo-Kleinian traditions elucidated in chapter 5.

The marginalisation of psycho-dynamic concepts within psychology may be short lived. Contemporary neuro-psychological work on emotions has revitalised many early psycho-dynamic ideas. Interestingly, the neuro-psychologist LeDoux (1998) draws heavily upon early psychoanalytic work to explain the emotional system. He provides a renewed impetus within psychology for the study of unconscious processing. As a corollary of his interest in fear, he theorises anxiety, drawing heavily on Freudian tenets. For example, he defines anxiety as 'a brooding fear of what might happen' (LeDoux, 1998: 130) and distinguishes it from fear in terms of the lack of external stimulus required to elicit anxiety. Anxiety comes from within. He links it, primarily, to a memory of a fearful event, which gets lodged in the unconscious. Anxiety-related aspects of early experience get stored in memory systems which are not directly accessible to consciousness. This makes the stored material highly resistant to change. It exerts its influence throughout the life of the human. This concept is highly compatible with the Kleinian idea that responses to anxiety in the paranoid-schizoid position leave traces on responses to anxiety which recur throughout the lifespan (see chapter 5). The brooding fear, the dread of what might happen, rather than dangers which have already struck, forms the focus of this book.

Contemporary neuro-psychology and psychoanalysis make interesting bedfellows. The revitalisation of the older tradition may usher in exciting insights for both disciplines. One of the valuable contributions of neuro-psychology is its ability to theorise the separateness of emotion and cognition. Work on human and animal brains shows that, when damaged, certain regions make for a loss in emotional appraisal but not a loss of cognitive capacities. In addition, such work shows that the emotional meaning of a stimulus can begin to be appraised before the perceptual systems have fully processed the stimulus. Consequently 'It is, indeed, possible for your brain to know that something is good or bad before it knows exactly what it is' (LeDoux, 1998: 69). These are dramatic findings, which contradict core tenets of cognitive psychology.

The new focus on emotion in neuro-psychology and sociology provide fascinating insights. Yet the challenge is to link the processes they elucidate to the subjective realm. How do people experience their own emotions? Factors in the psychic development of the infant impact upon how emotions are experienced. Similarly, the external environment, with its prescriptions concerning which emotions and emotional styles are appropriate, must shape emotional life. Emotional life, in origin and in everyday occurrence, is essentially relational. The early interaction with the primary caregiver determines the degree of loving attachment to others which individuals feel as well as the modes of response to anxiety. These modes of response or representations are moulded, in the course of the lifespan, by cultural input which is not always accessible via individual minds. The imperative to protect the self from imminent danger is primary. It is no wonder, then, that representations of risks are structured around self and in-group protective processes.

NOTES

1 LeDoux's theory bears a degree of similarity to William James' earlier ideas in that both give primacy to the physiological aspect of emotion. Within the Jamesian strand of emotions research people's sense of their bodily reactions to an emotion-eliciting stimulus *is* or *produces* the emotion. For example, butterflies in the stomach when facing a large audience produces a feeling of anxiety, rather than the feeling of anxiety, when facing this audience, producing the physical responses, as everyday thinking holds. So the feedback from the body produces the feeling aspect of emotion. Despite the difference in status of the scientific findings that each has access to, strands of Le Doux's thinking resemble those of James.

2 This flaw in the research measure can arise in even the most rigorously piloted studies, since the most frequently elicited, spontaneously occurring responses may be generated by a small proportion of the pilot group. Yet the responses which are generally chosen for inclusion in a final study are selected on the basis that they are the most frequently occurring responses (see Haddock *et al.*, 1993).

3 Later in the developmental process such representations transform and encompass a more complex view of both self and other (see chapter 8).

4 The cognitive unconscious (see Kihlstrom, 1987) accounts for 'subterranean processes' that go on outside of conscious awareness and undertake the mind's everyday functioning. This concept is similar to implicit processing. Cognitive measures, such as reaction times, are used to tap them.

5 At the very core of discursive psychology is the discouragement of speculation about 'inner states', and the adoption of discourse analytic methods to study discursive interaction. Recently, authors such as Billig (1997) have suggested a reconciliation of discursive and Freudian psychoanalytic theories. Billig

claims that the verbal level needs to be perused for what is not said, rather than what is said. A polite utterance, for example, necessarily represses a more rude impulse. This reconciliation may provide useful methods.

6 Ekman *et al.* (1987) showed that people from a vast range of countries – including Western, non-Western and non-literate cultures – interpret the facial expressions depicted in a set of photographs in the same way. The study included: happiness, sadness, fear, disgust, anger and surprise. The researchers claimed that there is a universal set of facial expressions which refer to specific emotions. Like the neuro-psychological literature, the facial expressions literature emphasises the evolutionary survival quality of emotions and all emotions are deemed to be combinations or modifications of the primary set (Ekman 1984, 1992). Mapped onto these basic emotions are certain behavioural patterns, such as protective behaviour being associated with fear. This relates back to the function of emotions as survival mechanisms.

If people worried constantly about the plethora of risks that might face them each day, life would be intolerable. The sense of invulnerability to potential danger is adaptive. Indeed, I have shown that there is a link between a high level of optimism regarding risks and better mental well-being, and evidence for a positive relationship between optimism and the ability of one's immune system to fight off illness. However, the 'not me – others' response to epidemics, wars and many other risks leaves people open to being affected by them, because the feeling of invulnerability may decrease people's chances of taking precautions against coming into contact with them. This makes the 'not me – other' response an issue of grave concern for those responsible for controlling levels of risk taking in a society. In light of the explanations which I have put forward for the 'not me – others' response, can it be modified? Are deep-seated, defensive responses to imminent danger inevitable?

Are representations of risks changeable?

Can risks be represented without blaming 'the other'? Must a polluting 'other' be represented as the harbinger of disaster? Strands of anthropological and cultural theory display profound scepticism concerning the possibility that social representations of risks can be changed. From this vantage point, 'the other' and risk are inextricably linked since deep-seated, defensive responses to danger protect communities, groups and selves from potential chaos. Douglas (1990) attests to the unchangeability of the response to threats over time in her notion that risk is merely old-fashioned danger dressed in modern clothes. Responses to it have been continuous over time. Crucially, regarding the issue of the modification of responses to risks, Douglas (1992) argues that since danger is important for the protection of the public good, it cannot be diminished by a call to reason. She states that the legacy of the rationalist tradition, which she rejects, lies in the belief that increased awareness

126

decreases magical thinking. For her, this level lives on regardless of attempts to minimise and to control it.

By way of contrast, psycho-dynamic thinking's central tenet relates to the very call to reason. This is paradoxical since psychoanalysis is a discipline centrally concerned with the workings of the unconscious, a place from which non-rational facets of psychic life emanate. People are deemed to be strangers unto themselves, to their inner psychic life. Control cannot readily be exerted on this realm of experience. However, psychoanalysis is a discipline forged within the rationalistic tradition. The practice of psychoanalysis's *raison d'être* is to build up a relationship between the unconscious and consciousness, between unreason and reason. This discipline forms a key part of the Enlightenment project, which expounded a view of the self which could be subject to control, planning and ordering. A goal of psychoanalysis is to facilitate self-control and rational action in its recipients. Rustin (1995) suggests that Freud's insistence that unconscious aspects of the mind could be understood is a manifestation of the self-confidence of European rationalism, related to the Enlightenment. Freud's work formed a part of the nineteenth-century tendency which endeavoured to probe all aspects of the natural world with scientific methods. He aimed to use such methods to help humankind deal with the terror of the unknown (Elliott and Frosh, 1995). By making the non-rational known, by allowing it to be symbolised, meaning could be made from it.

This orientation is compatible, epistemologically, with aspects of social representations theory. Both are modernist theories which explore how meaning is made of the 'messy' set of phenomena that people encounter in their lives. One of the primary aims of social representations theory is to explain how order is imposed on new occurrences. This is accomplished by linking them with already familiar phenomena and with symbols that circulate in the culture. People are driven by a need for a safe, stable vision of the universe, a status quo at the level of representation. A fear of, and the need to overcome, threats to the psyche are common to both social representations and psychoanalytic theories. The impetus to make order is driven by emotional needs, in both perspectives. Both theories are concerned with people's unease regarding the unknown. They are not centrally concerned with how people distort material 'realities' in their thoughts, as one finds in mainstream cognitive theories. Neither deny the 'real' material level. However, rather than the error-prone, faulty readers of reality, there is a focus on the lenses through which people look at and thereby construct their universes. The lens is tinted by a worldview set up in infancy, but open to modification by experience. The progeny of these united theories forms an invaluable framework for theorising subjective responses to mass risks.

The workings of change

How can people develop a sense of vulnerability, rather than invulnerability, to crises? Firstly, within a psychoanalytic approach, the developmental process, in itself, can create a self which does not project onto others, thereby leaving the self with a sense of invulnerability at times of crisis. Alternatively, psychoanalysis offers a means of repairing a psyche not able to move away from a split worldview. I peruse both ways of reaching representations which lack the blaming of 'the other' and refer to the parallel process, at a societal level, which fosters non-blaming reactions.

The first position, the paranoid-schizoid position, develops the infant's capacity to order chaos by splitting 'good' from 'bad' objects and experiences, at the level of representation. Based upon observational studies, Klein (1952) posits that following on from this position, at approximately the age of 6 months, infants move into the 'depressive position' in which the ability to tolerate ambivalence develops. The second and final position in the psychic development of the infant is the one in which the capacity to deal with anxiety in a non-split way develops. Within this position the infant realises that both nourishment and deprivation, satisfaction and persecution, derive from the same primary object. It reconciles the polarisation between 'good' and 'bad' experiences and objects, which had been established in the earlier stage of development, when it begins to mourn the loss of the 'purely good' self and the 'purely good' primary object, realising that 'bad' is contained within both. If mourning takes place, the infant is said to have entered the depressive position in which it acquires an ability to tolerate ambivalence. This is central to a non-split way of viewing the world. The most basic of defences against anxiety is to be found in the paranoid position in which the infant oscillates between the unlinked experiences of hate and love. Yet when it moves into the depressive position it begins to worry, to engage with the idea that the hate will destroy the good and this sends the individual on a path towards non-idealised representations. The newfound ambivalence allows the infant to represent both itself and others in terms of a complex set of feelings. To be emotionally ambivalent is to be able to hold, simultaneously, positively and negatively charged feelings. This is particularly difficult for the developing psyche since it must link and reconcile states which have previously been held apart to defend the core of the self. Complex, rather than simplistic and polarised, perceptions of an event become possible.

It is important to reiterate that Kleinian theory places little emphasis upon the 'real' interaction between caregiver and infant.[1] The focus is on the representational life of the infant: it is at the moment when the infant can apprehend the primary caregiver as a whole rather than as a number of part objects, some of which are nurturing and others depriving, that it enters the depressive position. Both the paranoid and depressive positions are encountered in the first year of life, and subsequent emotional life oscillates between the two (Allingham, 1987). These facets of emotional life are crucial in theorising responses to potential risks since they indicate that finding enemies outside of ourselves at times of threat need not occur. Both the proclivity for splitting and for tolerating ambivalence exist in adult representations, although there are variable levels of these states in different individuals. The successful entry into the second position of development explains why projection is not evident in all representations of the impending crisis. Kleinian theory accounts for the ability, which rests within most people, to view the world in a non-split way. The acquisition of mental tools with which to think in terms of more complex categories allows the individual to tolerate differing perspectives and contradictions.

The emphasis on only the first phase of Kleinian development, as can be detected in the work of Gilman (1985a, 1988), Crawford (1994) and the social theorists who allude only to the splitting mechanism, truncates object relations theory. It reifies the early part of development, abstracting it from later transformations. These later developments have explanatory power in terms of the existence of a lack of monolithically punitive thinking in the face of the majority of dangers. They assist in the explanation of why not everyone states 'not me – others' when faced with risks. Alluding to illness threats, Radley (1999) shows that theory which focuses on the exclusion of stigmatised groups overlooks the compassion which is regularly shown towards those who suffer. Compassion is so severely under-represented in the social scientific literature on illness because it does not appear to fit with the ideology of individualism. Within such an ideology people are said to operate on the basis of purely selfish motives, yet, for Radley, this focus leaves out a more complex picture in which a care ethos is germane. Similarly, I noted that victims of the Gulf War were symbolised in a sympathetic manner by a sample of Europeans. This is useful since it shows that people hold a complex array of responses to 'outsiders' rather than purely negative representations. This fits with the more ambivalent, complex relational element which develops in the depressive position, and, to varying degrees, is latent in most people. However, it also needs to be remembered that sympathy tends to accompany attributions in which the people who are being judged are seen to have become victims of the misfortune through no fault of their own (see chapter 4). As soon as choice and control are implicated in the person having come to harm, blame enters. Members of Western societies, in particular, imagine that others bring misfortunes upon themselves and this militates against sympathetic responses.

When people fail to move into the developmental task in which polarised phenomena come to be seen in terms of 'grey areas', interventions can be used to change the course of the split representations. In clinical terms, the interaction with a qualified analyst enables people to change their patterns of response to threatening events. Psychoanalysis advocates the healing potential of self-knowledge. A long-term, intensive liaison between psychoanalyst and patient facilitates the development of self-knowledge which, in terms of the modernist project, allows for change. The project of change advocated by Klein and her followers has as its starting point the idea that there is a need to take the patient's inner emotional states as matters of reflection. It focuses on the recognition of the mental pain and anxiety that patients feel and which manifest when patients engage in free association. The analyst is careful not to judge what the patient says, but merely to observe, to take interest and to point out the links that the pathways of the patient's own thinking throw up. The goal is to foster a self which is sufficiently robust to experience and to tolerate strong, often unpleasant feelings without acting upon them immediately or blindly. It is a self with a firm sense of its own boundaries. It knows what lies outside and what lies inside (Craib, 1990). Therefore it comes to recognise, and to take responsibility for, its own projections. Though perceived as determinist, a psychoanalytic vantage point offers a more flexible vision of how change in the projective processes, roused by anxiety, can be brought about. The reintegration of early emotions and defences, within the conscious part of the self, allows for the possibility of transforming existing representations rather than having their effects occur through unconscious processes. Provided by a trained analyst, it allows material from the unknown territory of the unconscious to be linked to conscious, everyday experience and behaviour, over which control can be exerted.

There are societal processes which give individuals self-knowledge in a manner analogous to the clinical level of intervention. These processes are relevant to responses to the anxiety evoked by mass risks. The project of change, suggested by psychoanalysts, contains similar elements to the more sociological concept of reflexivity. This is the 'susceptibility of most aspects of social activity . . . to chronic revision in the light of new information' (Giddens, 1991:20). Reflexivity, which grows as the mass media and academia produce explanations and commentaries related to the multiple facets of social life, contributes to the modification of the ideas which have persisted from a less reflexive past. Of course it might be argued that the unconscious level can be reached only in a more intimate, clinical communication (see chapter 5). Yet the concept of replacing unreason with reason may, at some level, be akin to the reflexive process. In addition, among the academic commentators who feed the process, are psycho-dynamically informed theorists who, by definition, commentate on and thereby impact upon non-conscious elements of experience.

The response to AIDS in Britain provides a demonstration of the shift that can occur in representations of a crisis over time. While I have shown that the initial response to the crisis was the formation of representations which projected perversity outward onto foreigners, out-groups and alien practices, the representations have moved to a more ambivalent position, to the more tempered representations which exist in relation to chronic illnesses (e.g. Berridge, 1992). This process has occurred across many cultures (see Fee and Fox, 1992). It has been fed by the power of the gay voice, which has challenged the dominant social representations. In addition, academic commentary, has highlighted how the danger posed by AIDS has led to society's 'others' becoming the targets of blame. Modifications in lay representations have ensued from such challenges. This is not to say that the sense of distance from the risk, the sense of subjective immunity, does not survive. Yet a more conscious, reasoned response can overlay and challenge the more immediate response. In addition, the threat posed by AIDS, at a material level, has receded in the West as a consequence of the advent of drugs which prevent people with HIV from acquiring the AIDS-related symptoms. Since anxiety in relation to the threat underpins the defensive process, a diminished threat reduces the need for defensive protection.

The outcome of the reflexivity provided by clinicians or by social commentators is that unconscious emotional life is given conscious voice, and so knowledge and reason can impact upon it. People learn to live without an idealised sense of self and without seeing others as enemies. When polarisation is no longer a tenable model, one has to turn to resolving the splits within, to reflect upon one's own fears, one's own perverse and abhorrent parts. Rather than viewing the 'other' as a recipient of just desserts, a participant in sin cocktails, the victim of the hazard is merely a person who was at the wrong place at the wrong time.

Paradoxically, while Kleinian theory is often criticised for its emphasis on an innately destructive inner self, it emerges as the more transformative of the available theories on the response to threat. Psychic integration, an enhanced capacity for recognition of the mixture of 'good' and 'bad' aspects within the self and within others, can be nurtured. Rustin (1995) terms the Kleinian paradigm a 'positive' model of the self since it contains a propensity for constructive and creative, as well as for destructive and perverse, representations. It is a model of a self (or ego) which can be developed and channelled in a more constructive direction. Rustin juxtaposes this positive model with Lacan's framework in which a sense of self-identity is based on 'lack', a lack which cannot be repaired in symbolic or imaginary terms and leaves the individual with a permanent sense of alienation. This aspect of the self is fixed. As in Freudian theory, Klein assumes that the unconscious aspects of the mind are understandable and that by bringing the interaction of internal and external dynamics to consciousness, change can be enacted. The very idea of changeability must be cherished when set against not only the more rigid sense of self that some psychodynamic thinkers propose, but the growing phalanx of theories about the fixed genetic predispositions and brain structures that control emotional life.[2]

Restating how the 'not me – other' model operates

Having encompassed the key aspects of psycho-dynamic and social representations theory which I seek to integrate, I am now in a position to outline my 'not me – other' model of the response to mass risks. In order to ascertain why the 'not me', 'not my group', 'others are to blame' representation has developed and is present in both past and contemporary responses to risks, a focus upon the mechanisms of response to anxiety in the first years of life is particularly illuminative. Splitting, introjection, projection and projective identification are among the first active mental processes of the infant. These primary mental processes are orientated towards keeping 'bad' objects away from 'good' objects. The 'bad' is associated with others, onto whom they are projected, while the 'good' is introjected into the self. Human mental processes are built upon an inner-structure which strives to distinguish between a 'good' self and a 'bad' other. Early splitting defences become a part of the vicissitudes of everyday interaction. They are rekindled when individuals experience helplessness in relation to objects in the external world. The emphasis, from a Kleinian standpoint, is not upon people who split as opposed to those who do not, as if splitting were a trait. Rather, relics of such mechanisms exist in all people, to varying degrees, and the mechanisms can be exacerbated by renewed threats to the self in concert with the extent to which representations in the social environment allay or exacerbate this polarising tendency.

In keeping with the work of cultural theorists such as Gilman (1985a, 1985b, 1988) and Crawford (1994), I suggest that the splitting process occurs when faced with disasters and that although it may occur internally, it gets articulated via the social terrain in which the child and then the adult finds some elements already symbolised as 'good' and associated with the self and the in-group, and others lying outside of this space of purity, ready to absorb unwanted thoughts and feelings. Representations that circulate in the social environment play a central role in the social representations that form in the minds of lay thinkers. This is an assumption in Gilman's work, and is borne out empirically in my own (see chapter 3). If the scientific, mass media and political realms present the issue in a polarised fashion, the social environment can be said to be intensifying the splitting process. If risks are associated with 'the other' in the external environment, we can expect that parallel processes will occur within lay thinking. A useful illustration of the melding of subjective feelings and the social environment emerges from a study of levels of xenophobia in East German youth at the time of the transition:

Xenophobia itself can be a private affair, but it is the public management of threat and blame that raises and lowers the level of political xenophobia in a society. The specific case of East German youth suggests that a sense of threat is the single most important element in the link, but also that the convergence of threat with proto-ideological elements of the right produce the highest levels of political xenophobia. In East Germany at the time of the transition (*Wende*), this convergence effect produced particularly high levels of political xenophobia among young males.' (Watts, 1996: 122)

The focus on the period in infancy in which the individual fails to experience a sense of a boundary between itself and that which is outside of it provides insight into how threat is represented. Confusion regarding whether destructive feelings lie inside or outside of the self is evident in the projective identification in which people represent objects outside of themselves in terms of their own unresolved issues. Such objects then become dangerous and powerful in the minds of the representors, evoking a sense of paranoia against which representors feel they must protect themselves. Xenophobia, other prejudices and stereotyping result.

In theorising the response to crises, there is a need to emphasise the role of representation rather than 'real' interactions with others.

Individual minds contain proclivities towards certain types of social representations at times of raised anxiety. Extreme conditions, especially those characterised by potential loss and change, jeopardise the sense of mastery over a known universe, confronting individuals with the potential to be drawn into a sphere of chaos. Throughout history, disasters have shaken up the fabric of societies, impacting upon demographic and moral systems. It is against the backdrop of such remembrances that individuals respond to mass risks. It is at the point when people feel most menaced by a danger that a split representation returns from the earliest developmental stage. The very act of social representation formation is related to a fear of powerlessness in the face of a social object which cannot be held under one's control. Therefore the act of representation is a defensive one, it is an attempt to control a potentially uncontrollable universe. In representing an aspect of this universe in a split way, one not only forges a safe vision of it, but also unifies with others who hold similar representations, thereby allaying the fear of isolation and fragmentation which also originate in the earliest years of life (Kaes, 1984).

I have reiterated the workings of the splitting mechanism at times of raised anxiety. This mechanism lies at the heart of many of the theories which allude to the projective thinking that arises at times of crisis. Yet this needs to be tempered by the feelings and defences that come into play in the second position of development. It is in recognition of this second position that I diverge from Gilman's and Crawford's theories. The key point of divergence lies in these cultural models being more 'negative' in that they imply a more fixed nature of blaming responses. My concern is to uncover the aspects of psycho-dynamic and social theory which allow for the development of a pathway towards changing social representations of risks. In Klein's depressive position, the capacity to reconcile polarised visions of self and other is developed, with the result that a less idealised view of self, and a less denigrated view of the other, is produced. The more complex orientation towards events which develops is neglected in cultural theory's understandings of representations of threats. The potential changeability of representations, which results both from fostering (either developmentally or analytically) individuals' ability to see the world in non-polarised terms and from social commentaries which contain this more complex vision, has a number of implications. It provides cause for hope since the deleterious effects of the splitting representation can be avoided. The 'not me – others' representations, which stem from the paranoid-schizoid phase, subject their victims to abuse of a verbal, physical and legal nature. They also contribute to an internalisation of a spoiled identity on the part of those who become the repositories for the unwanted material. In addition, the subjective sense of immunity to a crisis, on the part of the 'projectors', leaves them vulnerable to the effects of the crisis. This manifests in people who fail to practise safer sex because they associate AIDS with out-groups, or who fail to take precautions in relation to industrial or nuclear accidents, wars, hurricanes or volcanoes, because they represent the risk in a way that discounts the danger posed to themselves.

The optimistic bias literature shows that myriad health and safety risks evoke a response in which peers are perceived to be more likely to be affected by negative events than the self. Its explanation of why this occurs, like that within cultural theory, promotes a fairly unchangeable vision of the optimistic thinker. The optimistic response results from errors in information processing. People's lack of experience with the risk makes it difficult to imagine how it might affect them. Alternatively, people may compare themselves with others who are at particularly high risk in order to maintain a sense of low personal risk. They may also overestimate the skills that they have which would allow them to avoid being affected. These cognitive tricks are intrinsic to people upholding their positive sense of self-esteem, according to cognitive psychologists. If patterns of thinking about risks are thought to be essential for the maintenance of positive self and/or in-group identity, conceiving of mechanisms to change them is difficult. This pertains to anthropological and cultural theory too, in which apprehension of risks is intricately tied in to protection of the group or community. Of course, the psycho-dynamic notion of the adaptiveness of defensive responses implies a similar motive. The life force informs this. Yet the very aim of the psychodynamic approach is to penetrate the defensive armour, in the belief that this sets up a more robust, more integrated and complex self.

Critiques of psychoanalysis and social representations theory

Originally I turned to psychoanalytic theories because I was unable to explain the themes that arose in my AIDS study using existing social representations concepts exclusively. Kleinian theory, in particular, offered a way of looking at the remarkably similar trends which I found cross-culturally in my empirical work, and which I later realised existed in cross-disciplinary data on a diverse array of risks. It allowed me to analyse what underpins the mirrored 'not me – others' responses to myriad risks which exist in so many groups and cultures.

However, use of this type of theorisation by social psychologists has the potential to evoke strong criticism from psychoanalytic, social scientific and psychological circles. The psychoanalyst might object to the appropriation, by social theorists, of clinically derived findings (see chapter 5). However, such objections are not manifold. In fact, a number of prominent Kleinian psychoanalysts have, themselves, extrapolated from the clinical work into the social realm. Hannah Segal's (1995) work on responses to nuclear threat provides a key example. In addition, a group concerned with psychoanalysis's link to the public sphere has a strong presence in Britain.[3]

From the social scientific perspective, Freudian thought, and psychoanalytic concepts more generally, have been criticised for disregarding broad social factors in focusing upon the formation of individual psyches. Lupton (1997) states that since contemporary sociology is primarily concerned with inter-subjectivity – the relations of individuals with others, the impact of social structures on individuals and their behaviour – it is less attentive to how people experience the world via their 'individualised biographies' and via inner, not necessarily rational or conscious forces. Postmodern currents within the social sciences, in particular, eschew the notion of intra-psychic structures, and therefore tend to be highly opposed to psycho-dynamic concepts.

Of course there are many different ways of thinking about postmodernity but utilising Michael's (1994: 396) definition: 'The "modernist" individual is: "self-controlled", discrete, orderly, unitary . . . possessed of a powerful sense of place and the "Other". The postmodern is: "uncontrolled", multiplicitous, transgressive, decentred . . . possessed of a weak sense of place and sensitized to "others".' I hope to have demonstrated, throughout the book, that the orientation of most people seems to lie more with the qualities that Michael (1994) associates with modernism, rather with those he identifies with postmodernism. I find little evidence for these postmodern currents either in terms of the apprehension of risk or in terms of emotional life.

At the other end of the social scientific spectrum, however, lies a growing band of cultural theorists and sociologists who ascribe to the need for a theory of subjectivity and choose psychoanalytic concepts over cognitivist strands of psychology. I have mentioned Gilman and Crawford's work in this regard, but Giddens' (1992) work also reflects this trend. In addition, using certain arguments which overlap with my own, Lupton (1997) calls for bringing Kleinian and Freudian psychoanalytic theory back into medical sociology.

Anglo-American psychologists frequently dismiss psychoanalytic concepts, seeing them as relics of an antiquated paradigm. This is captured by a passing comment made by a psychologist reviewing a recent book on hysteria. He says of the writer: 'She displays an uncritical acceptance of Freudian beliefs, and ways of thought, an act of faith now virtually confined to novelists and literary critic, both professions more interested in a good "narrative" than the truth' (Sutherland, 1997: 239). Even though its findings are gleaned from clinical evidence, followed by considerable deliberation rather than 'uncritical acceptance', psycho-analytic thinking tends to be regarded as akin to 'armchair philosophy'. The fundamental scepticism stems from its method of gleaning know-ledge. This criticism is also levelled at social representations research (see Farr, 1996). Both are regarded as unscientific. I shall return to the issue of what good science is, having reviewed some of the other critiques of social representations theory.

The concept 'social representation' has been deemed problematic both in terms of being too broad and in terms of its tautological rather than linear assumptions (Fife-Shaw, 1997). The two claims are interlinked. According to Fife-Shaw's argument, since social represen-tationalists claim that thought and action express underlying represen-tations, everything can be subsumed under the notion of social representation: 'almost any data could be used to assert the existence of a social representation about anything' (Fife-Shaw, 1997: 69). The accusation is that a lack of linear, predictive theorising exists in the theory: 'Social representations cause both thought and action and *are* thought and action' (ibid.). It needs to be restated that in the strand of the tradition to which I ascribe, proof of causality is not a goal. Constellations of representations are hypothesised to underpin, but not to cause, thought and action. One may construe a model in which circularity is recognised – representations feed thought/action and thought/action feed representations – as tautological (see Potter and Litton, 1985). Yet one may also construe it as a reciprocal model, rather than a linear one. An example lends substance to this claim. It seems highly plausible that the social representation of individuals as entities who are responsible for the outcomes which befall them, in Western society, goes some way to explaining why blaming attitudes arise in relation to many risks. Yet such representa-tions do not *cause* the attributions. They are merely the culturally transmitted, taken-for-granted (or tacit) assumptions which play a part in structuring how individuals explain their worlds. The attribu-tions also influence the representational process, making it impossible to posit a cause–effect relationship. Since linear, causal models are dominant in psychology, non-predictive models appear flawed. However, social representations theory embodies a deliberate attempt to build up a complex model of common-sense thought which contains multiple, reciprocal influences.

Social representations theory has also been accused of doing little more than theories which already have a wide currency within psychology (Fife-Shaw, 1997). There *is* considerable overlap between social representations theory and understandings of lay theories which operate within social constructionist principles. These include certain renditions of interpretative phenomenological analysis (e.g see Smith *et al.*, 1997), interpretative repertoires (Wetherall and Potter, 1992) and rhetorical analysis (see Billig, 1987), among others. The data that emerge from research conceptualised within these frameworks can augment and complement one another. Yet social representations theory is distinctive, both from these and, particularly, from the empirically driven lay theory approach (e.g. Furnham, 1988). It differs in that its central concern is the transfer of information between social institutions and minds, with an additional emphasis upon the transfer of older ideas to new phenomena, and the emotively rooted symbolisation of new events in terms of existing metaphors and images in the particular culture in which they are being apprehended. A theory that focuses upon the uptake of scientific knowledge by the psyche, and the meanings formed there, has the potential to confront the challenges still faced within the preventive risk field. Meanings made of risks have not been addressed by information processing models which focus on the 'errors' that interfere with logical processing.

Mainstream psychology clings to notions of fixed, internal cognitions, to the view that the social context of thinking is inconsequential. Where contextual factors are acknowledged, and assigned a role in the cognitive models, their role tends to be inadequately theorised. For example, when the Theory of Reasoned Action and its offshoots are used, the respondent's 'normative beliefs / attitudes' are tapped. Yet this is measured by asking about the beliefs of family and friends pertaining to the issue under investigation. Even when the conceptualisation is widened to the influence of social institutions, no attempt is made to discern how the normative influences come to bear. In addition, in the optimistic bias model, comparison to 'others' generally involves comparison to peers of the same age and gender. There is some work which primes respondents to think in terms of in-groups and out-groups in both the optimistic bias and attribution literatures. Yet they are concerned with the lone thinker's subjective processing. If they were to look outside, into the social environment in which the thinker operates, they would be struck less by information-processing biases and errors and more by how the hallowed institution of science is as steeped in symbolic, 'error' filled meanings, at least at the point of initially attempting to discern the threat posed by new dangers, as their faulty human information processors are. They would be forced to study the communication of ideas between different spheres and to recognise that even scientific ideas are not clear-cut and 'objective'. Like lay ideas, they are tinged with emotive, value-based meanings.

Finally, since social representations theory cannot be proven wrong, in positivist terms 'it adopts the qualities of an article of faith', according to Fife-Shaw (1997: 69). This criticism has also been levelled at psychoanalysis. It is often heralded as a religion rather than a theory thereby occluding the clinical observation which forms the scientific basis of the tradition. Since most theories have a short shelf life, those which endure must, at the very least, find resonance with large numbers of theorists. The psyche does not tolerate all interpretations. It is not open to any conceivable explanation. Psycho-dynamic notions such as that of defensiveness, and of the loaded nature of jokes and dreams, has so pervaded Western culture that they are taken for granted. Of course this claim is less apt in regard to social representations theory, which has been in circulation since 1961. We have to wait and see whether it, or, at least, its emphasis upon communication and symbolisation, continues to contribute to the social sciences in generations to come.

What is good theory?

What are the necessary aspects of good, scientific theory? Social psychology is a social rather than a natural science. Therefore natural scientific models of good theory are inappropriate: 'It is an increasingly accepted view that work becomes scientific by adopting methods of study *appropriate* to its subject matter' (Silverman, 1993: 144, original italics). Let us briefly peruse some of the assumptions of the natural science model so as to indicate its unsuitability for the study of the 'not me – others' response.

An important aspect of a theory, within natural science, of which mainstream psychology sees itself as a branch, is that it generates predictions which can be tested. If they are falsified, the theory is changed and the relationships between further variables tested. The aim of knowledge, within this framework, is to establish truths, to set up fixed laws based upon causal relationships between phenomena. This is antithetical to the notion of reciprocal relationships between variables which is part and parcel of social representations theory. The notion of 'truth' is also problematic from the more social constructionist perspective since my very argument is that people look upon 'true risks' through

lenses tinged with elements of unconscious thought, of group attachment and of the experiences of such groups in the past. These elements
do not distort a 'real risk'. Rather, they *are* the 'reality' in the minds of
those who look upon the risks.

This throws up the issue of how one establishes such a theory. One
cannot rely upon observed relationships between phenomena. Observation depends upon the accessibility of phenomena to the senses. Yet the
most interesting aspects of risk-related responses, from my perspective,
are not readily accessible. Since cognitions are ideas one can call to
consciousness, they can be put into words, at least to some extent
(Allingham, 1987). However, ideas that one is unaware of are experienced indirectly rather than through words. Evidence for indirectly
experienced material, such as defensive responses, must be inferred.
Not only is psychoanalytic theory rooted in unobservable, unconscious
processes, but also the meanings that make up a social representation
are not manifest in the way that attitudes are. Yet these meanings
provide understanding of what underpins responses to risks. Jaspars and
Fraser (1984: 122) point out that: 'A much better understanding [of
human thought] can be achieved if we go beyond the manifest responses
which Ss provide in many attitude surveys and concern ourselves with
the representations which are implicit in these responses' (my emphasis). Questions concerning implicit meaning and unconscious defensiveness are not amenable to falsifiability.

Of course, in many social representational and psycho-dynamic
studies access to these levels are inferred via verbal material.[4] In
Hollway and Jefferson's (1997) model of the research process, talk is
assumed to reveal these deeper processes. Pathways of talk, forged by
respondents, reveal their unconscious associations. They are presumed
to be driven by emotional rather than rational motivations.

In order to explore the 'not me' response one needs to utilise social
scientific, rather than natural scientific premises. A key tenet of
positivism is that the natural sciences form the prototype for all
scientific inquiry, and that phenomena under study be observable via
the senses (see Marks, 1996; Stainton-Rogers, 1996; Yardley, 1997;
Ussher, 1996, for further, extensive critiques of the positivist model).
This is highly problematic for the study of the blaming responses
which arise at times of imminent danger since they are more amor-
phous than physical laws such as gravity. By definition, there is no
direct evidence of the existence of dynamic unconscious processing,
even though the 'not me – others' response cannot otherwise be fully
explained. Social representations are also intangible, yet epidemics
such as that of AIDS have demonstrated that groups share very specific

ideas about new threats, which cannot be explained without recourse to the social construction of reality.

When the questions asked of data are not amenable to direct observation, there are alternative ways of judging the utility and accuracy of fit of a theory. For Silverman (1993) social science must produce knowledge systematically. If it is merely constituted by a set of accounts, a set of interpretative studies, with no claims to reliability or validity, it is of little use. The general principles of reliability and validity must be built into social scientific work. The stability of the 'not me – others' phenomenon over time, and its manifestation across a range of groups, cultures and risks, within contemporary times, provides an indicator of the reliability of the findings. The validity of the theory is connected to this. Validity is assessed by whether the 'not me – others' response is plausible and credible, given our existing knowledge. The comparison of the different kinds of data, or triangulation, suggests plausibility in light of the body of work in the social sciences. The phenomenon appears to be robust in that different methods and theoretical standpoints, within various disciplines, corroborate one another. Examination of art, medical textbooks, scientific journals and interview material all reveal the portrayal of the 'other' in a degraded manner, with the heightening of this phenomenon at times of raised mass anxiety. Findings in cultural theory, anthropology, sociology and social psychology endorse one another.

Allingham (1987) makes complementary assertions to those of Silverman (1993) concerning good theory. He commences with the assumption that any model, and the theory based upon it,[5] is limited. Since we cannot observe the mind, we need a model of it. The purpose of the model is to simplify by omitting unimportant details. This distorts the picture to some extent but serves to explain or discover something that has not previously been fully understood. A 'good' model is internally consistent, that is, it stands as a logical whole. It is also externally consistent in that it accords with what we can infer about the workings of the mind. Finally, rather than being true or false, it is useful.

The possibility of forging an overarching theory concerning the response to risk

I advocate that there is a uniform element in the initial responses to all mass risks. I have shown that epidemics of the past and present, in both Western and non-Western contexts, have been associated with 'the other' of those who represent them. There is also a robust body of findings concerning the projection onto the other that occurs at times of economic crisis. Two points in German history have been mentioned: economic crises precipitated the genocide of Jews in Europe (see chapter 2) and, more recently, extreme levels of xenophobia concerning out-groups such as Turks. Further evidence of the 'not me' response is the denial of nuclear-related risk among those who live in dangerous proximity to nuclear reprocessing plants. Finally, in relation to the litany of health and safety risks which form a more constant feature of everyday life, such as those studied in the optimistic bias tradition, there is convincing evidence of the 'not me – other' response. Generalisation across these categories of risk, making a 'big picture' of these specific bodies of work, threatens to occlude the differing responses which each danger might provoke. However, I make the link by grounding myself in universal responses to anxiety which are latent in all of us, and became more salient under conditions of heightened fear. They are also more salient and more powerful in some individuals rather than others.

My overarching approach is antithetical to a strand of the risk literature in which divisions are made between 'natural' and 'manmade' disasters, as well as between risks and hazards. 'Natural' disasters include earthquakes, hurricanes and floods. 'Manmade' disasters are those produced abundantly in the 'risk society': nuclear and industrial accidents, the greenhouse effect, acid rain and so on. However, the division between natural and manmade danger is tenuous. This can be demonstrated with reference to the epidemic. Is it a natural or a manmade danger? In some senses it is 'natural' since its origins are often believed to relate to a mutation of an existing pathogen, at least in the medical scientific realm. However, people affected by epidemics tend to be seen as having brought them upon themselves – by a lack of hygiene, or by excesses in terms of sex, alcohol or drugs. I use this to indicate that risks tend to be conceptualised as if human choices were involved, whatever their material basis. Individual decisions tend to be implicated in some way. This factor diminishes the importance of the distinction between 'natural' and 'manmade' disasters, as well as that made between 'risks' and 'hazards'. The properties associated with the two sets of categories overlap substantially. Hazards tend to be distinguished from risks in that damage comes from an external source such as an aeroplane or brick landing upon one. The latter are said to become risks as soon as anything becomes known about how one might avoid the danger. On one level it is possible to distinguish between different types of danger: more volition is involved in having unsafe sex and contracting HIV than in dying as a result of a plane or meteorite crashing from the sky onto one. Yet the attributions theory literature confirms that there is a tendency to read volition into the actions of someone struck by a negative event, whatever the person's 'actual' role in coming into contact with it. I hope to have argued, by my emphasis on choice and intentionality, throughout the book, that risks have a 'manmade' element read into them, whatever their material basis.

Since so much effort has been expended on the scientific prediction of risks, in Western cultures, there is often information available concerning how one might prepare oneself, even for 'natural' disasters. Norris (1997) shows that people facing hazards such as hurricanes have a motto 'be prepared': large proportions of quota samples from southeastern, North American cities, where hurricanes are frequent, say that they keep a flashlight and extra batteries on hand, and are extremely careful about storing flammable materials. This motto, and these actions, may appear to contradict much of the thesis that I have set up. One might assume that the majority of these samples must feel vulnerable to hurricanes, otherwise they would not take these precautionary actions. Interestingly, Norris (1997) points out that underpinning both 'illusions of invulnerability' and taking precautionary behaviour, are people's convictions that tragedy and misfortune are preventable. Rather than being unconcerned about the management of risks, people facing the risk of hurricanes report that they act prepared. This self-reported action,[6] which minimises one's chances of becoming the victim of the risk, may accompany feelings of invulnerability[7].

Concluding remarks

I hope to have acknowledged and addressed the criticisms that have been levelled at the psychoanalytic and the social representational facets of my approach. An ongoing debate concerning this appeared in *British Journal of Medical Psychology* (see Joffe, 1996a; Fife-Shaw, 1997; Joffe, 1997b; Abraham *et al.*, 1998). I have also delved into the basis upon which I have chosen to generalise across risks and flagged up the criteria upon which the quality of my approach can be judged. In addition, a key aim of this chapter has been to address whether representations of risks can be changed. I have shown not only that there is a level at which unchanging residues from earlier phases impact on representations, but also that there is the possibility of transformation.

What lessons can be drawn from the discussion of the transformation of social representations, for intervention? I return briefly to AIDS, as a key example of a contemporary mass risk, in order to address this. There is ongoing and renewed bafflement, from the perspective of health policy-makers regarding the unsafe sex which many people have despite their networks being highly infected by HIV. Unlike the 'be prepared' ethos which is reflected in taking a flashlight along to reduce the danger which a hurricane may pose, risk behaviour continues unabated. Offir *et al.*'s (1993) finding that one-third of a North American sample of sexually active gay men report the frequent occurrence of unprotected sex, and that the vast majority of the sample had unsafe sex at least once since initiating condom use for the purpose of HIV risk reduction, is fairly typical of the results on gay men in the West. Drawing on assumptions about the power of knowledge to counter myth, governments devise prevention campaigns which aim to tell individuals the 'facts' in order to avert future risks. Lay people are supposed to process the 'facts' logically and to emerge with a realistic view of their own chances of coming into contact with the risk. The knowledge generated by science is assumed to allow for mastery of disasters. Yet the ongoing unsafe sex among groups in which levels of HIV and of HIV-related knowledge are high, and who are likely to have been exposed to many interventions targeted at changing their cognitions, suggest the need for a shift in approach.

I have shown by reference to a range of studies that monogamy is often used as the sole means of protection against HIV. Another form of protection is the choice of physically appealing partners: high sex appeal people are viewed as less risky regarding contracting STDs than low sex appeal people are (Blanton and Gerrard, 1997). It is important to highlight that while I deem these sets of meanings the *representation* of the partner, cognitive psychologists see them as 'cognitive heuristics' that distort risk perception. As a result of the cognitive framing of these meanings, theorists believe that if only more objective strategies of judging a partner could be fostered, safe sex would always occur. Malloy *et al.* (1997), for example, call for people to use more objective means of assessing their risks. They call for 'interventions aimed at moving individuals at risk from the strategy of attempting to "scope out" a partner's AIDS risk potential by using erroneous cognitive strategies to the vastly more effective strategy of adopting objectively effective AIDS preventive behaviours' (Malloy *et al.*, 1997: 485).

If one adopts a social representational stance, one talks of assessing partners in terms of their appearance and feelings of intimacy as lay logic, rather than 'erroneous cognitive strategy'. Entering the meaning systems of the people who practise these behaviours, researchers find that the partner who is let into the space of the self without protective barriers is the one construed as appealing and intimate. In a rather circular strand of lay reasoning, the 'good', healthy partner is the beautiful, familiar one. If one attempts to understand the response to risk purely cognitively one obfuscates its association with very powerful emotional states, as well as the larger cultural context in which behaviours are situated. Aspects of both emotion and culture are submerged in spaces beyond the conscious recognition of the individuals who are influenced by them. To reach them one requires more subtle understandings of how people apprehend risks than those currently produced.

Much early social psychology was directly concerned with the emotional life associated with mass movements, such as Adorno *et al.*'s (1950) work on the association between the emotional life of the authoritarian personality and fascism, and Le Bon's earlier (1895) work on the 'irrationality' of the crowd. The early concern with mass hysteria has given way to a concern with the mass or, more narrowly, the group, which has lost sight of the hysteria. It is the combination of social and emotional life, manifest in the individual's response to risk, which I hope to have reinvigorated in this book.

NOTES

1 However, Klein does allude to the fact that the presence of a 'real', loving mother can diminish the dread of the 'terrifying mother', particularly in the paranoid-schizoid phase. This line of reasoning has been developed in Winnicott's work (see Winnicott, 1958; Phillips, 1988).
2 However, it must be recognised that recent neuro-psychological findings point to plasticity of brain functioning. The brain may well remain 'plastic' throughout life, but particularly in the early years (see Goleman, 1996).
3 Its members tend to be drawn from the social sciences rather than from psychoanalytic circles, but there is an overlap between the two, in terms of social scientists who are also clinically trained.
4 There are ways in which the unconscious reveals the emotional life of the individual without words too. Psychosomatic symptoms, in particular, reveal part of the body 'thinking things through' (Phillips, 1995). These symptoms can be seen as ways of thinking and feeling through the body rather than through words.
5 The relationship between a theory and a model, according to Allingham (1987), is that a theory is a discourse about a model which hopes to translate key features of the model into rules and generalisations
6 Many such studies are based upon self-reports, and ask people about intended rather than actual behaviour.
7 Of course people's sense of invulnerability to risks may arise *because* they take the necessary precautions. However, I have flagged up an array of studies which indicate that the 'not me – other' representation does not, in general, correlate with safe behaviour.

References

Abraham, C., Sheeran, P. and Orbell, S. (1998). 'Can social cognitive models contribute to the effectiveness of HIV-preventive behavioural interventions? A brief review of the literature and a reply to Joffe (1996; 1997) and Fife-Shaw (1997)'. *British Journal of Medical Psychology*, 71: 297–310.

Adorno, T. W., Frenkel-Brunswick, E., Levison, D. J. and Sanford, R. N. (1950). *The authoritarian personality.* New York: Harper and Row.

Aggleton, P., Homans, H., Mojsa, J., Watson, S. & Watney, S. (1989). *AIDS: Scientific and social issues.* Edinburgh: Churchill Livingstone.

Agrafiotis, D. (1990). *Knowledge, attitudes, beliefs and practices of Athenians in relation to AIDS.* Report for World Health Organisation (WHO)/Global Programme on AIDS (GPA)/Social and Behavioural Research (SBR). Geneva: WHO.

Alcorn, K. (1989). 'AIDS in the public sphere: How a broadcasting system in a crisis dealt with an epidemic', in E. Carter & S. Watney (eds.) *Taking liberties: AIDS and cultural politics.* London: Serpent's Tail, pp. 193–212.

Alford, C. F. (1989). *Melanie Klein and critical social theory: An account of politics, art, and reason based on her psychoanalytic theory.* New Haven, CT: Yale University Press.

Allingham, M. (1987). *Unconscious contracts: A psychoanalytical theory of society.* London: Routledge.

Altman, D. (1986). *AIDS and the new puritanism.* London: Pluto.

Andreski, S. (1989). *Syphilis, puritanism and witch hunts.* London: Macmillan.

Averill, J. R. (1974/1996a). 'An analysis of psychophysiological symbolism and its influence on theories of emotion', in R. Harré and W. G. Parrott (eds.) *The emotions: Social, cultural and biological dimensions.* London: Sage, pp. 204–228.

  (1996b). 'Intellectual emotions', in R. Harré and W. G. Parrott (eds.), ibid., pp. 24–38.

  (1980). 'The emotions', in E. Staub (ed.) *Personality: Basic aspects and current research.* Englewood Cliffs, NJ: Prentice Hall, pp. 134–199.

Backett, E. M., Davies, A. M. and Petrof-Barvazian. (1984). The risk approach in health care. *Public Health Papers*, 76:1–113.

Bajos, N., Ducot, B., Spencer, B., Spira, A. and ACSF Group (1997). 'Sexual risk-taking, socio-sexual biographies and sexual interaction: Elements of the French national survey of sexual behaviour'. *Social Science and Medicine*, 44(1): 25–40.

Baker, G. W. and Chapman, D. W. (eds.) (1962) *Man and society in disaster*. New York: Basic Books.

Bar-Tal, D. (1990). *Group beliefs*. New York: Springer-Verlag.

Bauman, Z. (1993). *Postmodern ethics*. Oxford: Blackwell.

Beck, U. (1986/1992). *The risk society: Towards a new modernity*. London: Sage.

(1996). 'Risk society and the provident state', in S. Lash, B. Szerszynski and B. Wynne (eds.) *Risk, environment and modernity: Towards a new ecology*. London: Sage, pp. 27–43.

Beharrell, P. (1992). 'AIDS and the British press', in J. E. T. Eldridge (ed.) *Getting the message*. London: Routledge, pp. 210–249.

Benoit, D. and Parker, K. C. H. (1994). 'Stability and transmission of attachment across three generations'. *Child Development*, 65: 1,444–1,456.

Berridge, V. (1992). 'AIDS: History and contemporary history', in G. Herdt and S. Lindenbaum (eds.) *The time of AIDS: Social analysis, theory and method*. Newbury Park, CA: Sage, pp. 41–64.

Bettleheim, B. (1977). *The uses of enchantment*. New York: Vintage.

Billig, M. (1987). *Arguing and thinking: A rhetorical approach to social psychology*. Cambridge: Cambridge University Press.

(1997). 'The dialogic unconscious: Psychoanalysis, discursive psychology and the nature of repression'. *British Journal of Social Psychology*, 36: 139–159.

Bion, W. R. (1952). 'Group dynamics: A review'. *International Journal of Psycho-Analysis*, 33: 235–247.

(1961). *Experiences in groups*. London: Tavistock.

Blanton, H. and Gerrard, M. (1997). 'Effect of sexual motivation on men's risk perception for sexually transmitted disease: There must be 50 ways to justify a lover'. *Health Psychology*, 16(4): 374–379.

Blaxter, M. (1993). 'Why do the victims blame themselves?', in A. Radley (ed.) *Worlds of illness: Biographical and cultural perspectives on health and disease*. London: Routledge, pp. 124–142.

Bloor, D. (1976). *Knowledge and social imagery*. London: Routledge and Kegan Paul.

Bowlby, J. (1969). *Attachment and loss (vol. 1): Attachment*. New York: Basic Books.

(1973). *Attachment and loss (vol. 2): Separation, anxiety and anger*. New York: Basic Books.

Brandt, A. M. (1978). 'Racism and research: The case of the Tuskegee syphilis study'. *Hastings Center Report*, 8(21): 21–29.

Brown, J., Chapman, S. and Lupton, D. (1996). 'Infinitesimal risk as public health crisis: News media coverage of a doctor–patient HIV contact tracing investigation'. *Social Science and Medicine*, 43(12): 1,685–1,695.

Budescu, D. V. and Bruderman, M. (1995). 'The relationship between the illusion of control and the desirability bias'. *Journal of Behavioural Decision Making*, 8(2): 109–125.

Chapman, D. W. (1962). 'A brief introduction to contemporary disaster research', in G. W. Baker and D. W. Chapman (eds.) *Man and society in disaster*. New York: Basic Books, pp. 3–20.

Chirimuuta, R. & Chirimuuta, R. (1989). *AIDS, Africa and racism*. London: Free Association.

Cohn, N. (1976). *Europe's inner demons*. St Albans: Paladin.

Collins, H. M. (1985). *Changing order*. London: Sage.

Comaroff, J. (1982). 'Medicine: symbol and ideology', in P. Wright and A. Treacher (eds.) *The problem of medical knowledge: Examining the social construction of medicine*. Edinburgh: Edinburgh University Press, pp. 49–68.

Cornelius, R. R (1996). *The science of emotion*. Englewood Cliffs, NJ: Prentice Hall.

Craib, I. (1990). *Psychoanalysis and social theory*. Amherst: University of Massachusetts.

Crawford, R. (1977). 'You are dangerous to your health: The ideology and politics of victim blaming'. *International Journal of Health Services*, 7(4): 663–680.

(1984). 'A cultural account of "health" – control, release and the social body', in J. B. McKinlay (ed.) *Issues in the political economy of health care*. London: Tavistock, pp. 60–103.

(1994). 'The boundaries of the self and the unhealthy other: Reflections on health, culture and AIDS'. *Social Science and Medicine*, 38(10): 1,347–1,365.

Crossley, M. (1997). ' "Survivors" and "victims": Long-term HIV positive individuals and the ethos of self-empowerment'. *Social Science and Medicine*, 45(12): 1,863–1,873.

Crossley, N. (1998). 'Emotion and communicative action: Habermas, linguistic philosophy and existentialism', in G. Bendelow and S. J. Williams (eds.) *Emotions and social life: Critical themes and contemporary issues*. London: Routledge, pp. 16–38.

Dalton, H. L. (1989). 'AIDS and blackface'. *Daedalus*, 118(3): 205–227.

Davenport-Hines, R. (1990). *Sex, death and punishment*. London: Collins.

Davies, P. M., Hickson, F. C. I., Weatherburn, P. and Hunt, A. J. (1993). *Sex, gay men and AIDS*. London: Falmer.

Davison, C. (1996). 'Predictive genetics: The cultural implications of supplying probable futures', in T. Marteau and M. Richards (eds.) *The troubled helix: Social and psychological implications of the new human genetics*. Cambridge: Cambridge University Press, pp. 317–330.

Department of Health and Social Security (1976). *Prevention and health: Everybody's business*. London: HMSO.

Department of Health and Social Security and the Welsh Office (1987). *AIDS – Monitoring response to the public education campaign: February 1986 – February 1987*. London: HMSO.

Dijker, A. J., Koomen, W., van den Heuvel, H. and Frijda, N. H. (1996). 'Perceived antecedents of emotional reactions in inter-ethnic relations'. *British Journal of Social Psychology*, 35: 313–328.

Doane, J. and Hodges, D. (1992). *From Klein to Kristeva*. Ann Arbor: University of Michigan Press.

Doise, W., Clemence, A. and Lorenzi-Cioldi, F. (1993). *The quantitative analysis of social representations*. London: Harvester Wheatsheaf.

Douglas, M. (1966). *Purity and danger*. London: Routledge and Kegan Paul.

(1986). *Risk acceptability according to the social sciences*. London: Routledge.

(1990). 'Risk as a forensic resource. *Daedalus*, 119 (4): 1–16.

(1992). *Risk and blame: Essays in cultural theory.* London: Routledge.

Douglas, M. and Wildawsky, A. (1983). *Risk and culture.* Berkeley: University of California Press.

Douglas, T. (1995). *Scapegoats: Transferring blame.* London: Routledge.

Doyal, L. and Harris, R. (1986). *Empiricism, explanation and rationality: An introduction to the philosophy of the social sciences.* London: Routledge

Dunant, S. and Porter, R. (1996) 'Introducing anxiety', in S. Dunant and R. Porter (eds.) *The age of anxiety.* London: Virago, pp. ix–xviii.

Duveen, G. and Lloyd, B. (1990). 'Introduction', in G. Duveen & B. Lloyd (eds.) *Social representations and the development of knowledge.* Cambridge: Cambridge University Press, pp. 1–10.

Eckman, P. (1984). 'Expression and the nature of emotion', in K. Scherer and P. Eckman (eds.) *Approaches to emotion.* Hillsdale, NJ: Erlbaum.

(1992). 'Are there basic emotions?,' *Psychological Review*, 99: 550–553.

Eckman, P., Friesen, W. V., O'Sullivan, M., Chan, A., Diacoyanni-Tarlatzis, I., Heider, K., Krause, R., LeCompte, W. A., Pitcairn, T., Ricci-Bitti, P. E., Scherer, K. R., Tomita, M. and Tzavaras, A. (1987). 'Universals and cultural differences in the judgments of facial expressions of emotion'. *Journal of Personality and Social Psychology*, 53(4): 712–717.

Elliott, A. and Frosh, S. (eds.)(1995). *Psychoanalysis in contexts.* London: Routledge.

Fanon, F. (1992). 'The fact of blackness', in J. Donald and A. Rattansi (eds.) *'Race', culture and difference.* London: Sage, pp. 220–240.

Farmer, P. (1992). *AIDS and accusation: Haiti and the geography of blame.* Berkeley: University of California Press.

Farr, R. (1977). 'Heider, Harré and Herzlich on health and illness: Some observations on the structure of représentations collectives'. *European Journal of Social Psychology*, 7, (4): pp. 491–504.

(1987). 'Self/other relations and the social nature of reality', in C. Graumann & S. Moscovici (eds.) *Changing conception of conspiracy theory.* New York: Springer-Verlag, pp. 203–217.

(1996) *The Roots of Modern Social Psychology 1872–1954.* Oxford: Blackwell.

Fee, E. and Fox, D. M. (eds.)(1992). *AIDS: The making of a chronic disease.* Berkeley: University of California Press.

Feldman, D. A., O'Hara, P., Baboo, K. S., Chitalu, N. W. and Lu, Y. (1997). 'HIV prevention among Zambian adolescents: Developing a value utilization/norm change model'. *Social Science and Medicine*, 44(4): 455–468.

Fife-Shaw, C. (1997). 'Commentary on Joffe (1996) AIDS research and prevention: A social representations approach'. *British Journal of Medical Psychology*, 70: 65–73.

Flick, U. (1992). 'Triangulation revisited: Strategy of validation or alternative?' *Journal for the Theory of Social Behaviour*, 22(2): 175–197.

Fonagy, P., Steele, M., Moran, G., Steele, H. and Higgitt, A. (1993). 'Measuring the ghost in the nursery: An empirical study of the relationship between parents' mental representations of childhood experiences and their infants' security of attachment'. *Journal of the American Psychoanalytic Association*, 41(4): 957–989.

Frosh, S. (1989a). *Psychoanalysis and psychology.* London: Macmillan.

(1989b). 'Psychoanalysis and racism', in B. Richards (ed.) *Crises of the self: Further essays on psychoanalysis and politics*. London: Free Association, pp. 229–244.

Furnham, A. F. (1988). *Lay theories: Everyday understanding of problems in the social sciences*. Oxford: Pergamon.

Geertz, C. (1975) 'On the nature of anthropological understanding'. *American Scientist*, 63: p. 48.

Gerrard, M., Gibbons, F. X. and Bushman, B. J. (1996). 'Relation between perceived vulnerability to HIV and precautionary sexual behaviour'. *Psychological Bulletin*, 119(3): 390–409.

Geodert, J. J., Neuland, C. Y., Wallen, W. C., Greene, M. H., Mann, D. L., Murray, C. F., Strong, D. M., Fraumeni, J. F., & Blattner, W. B. (1982). 'Amyl nitrite may alter T-lymphocytes in homosexual men'. *Lancet* i: 412–415.

Giami, A. & Schiltz, M-A. (1996). 'Representations of sexuality and relations between partners: Sex research in France in the era of AIDS'. *Annual Review of Sex Research*, 7: 125–157.

Giddens, A. (1991). *Modernity and self-identity*. Cambridge: Polity.

(1992). *The transformation of intimacy*. Cambridge: Polity.

Gilbert, A. N. and Barkun, M. (1981). 'Disaster and sexuality'. *Journal of Sex Research*, 17(3): 288–299.

Gilman, S. (1985a). *Difference and pathology: Stereotypes of sexuality, race and madness*. Ithaca, NY: Cornell University Press.

(1985b). *Health and illness: Images of difference*. London: Reaktion.

(1988). *Disease and representation: Images of illness from madness to AIDS*. Ithaca, NY: Cornell University Press.

(1992). 'Black bodies, white bodies', in J. Donald & A. Rattansi (eds.) *'Race', culture and difference*. London: Sage, pp. 171–197.

Gilot, F. (1965). *Life with Picasso*. London: Nelson.

Ginsburg, G. P. and Harrington, M. E. (1996). 'Bodily states and context in situated lines of action', in R. Harré and W. G. Parrott (eds.) *The emotions: Social, cultural and biological dimensions*. London: Sage, pp. 229–258.

Gladis, M. G., Michela, J. L., Walter, H. J. and Vaughan, R. D. (1992). 'High school students' perception of AIDS risk: Realistic appraisal or motivated denial'. *Health Psychology*, 11(5): 307–316.

Gobineau, J. A. de (1856). *The moral and intellectual diversity of races, with particular reference to their respective incluence in the civil and political history of mankind*. Philadelphia, PA: Lippincott.

Goffman, E. (1963). *Stigma: Notes on the management of spoiled identity*. Harmondsworth: Penguin.

Goldin, C. S. (1994). 'Stigmatisation and AIDS: Critical issues in public health'. *Social Science and Medicine*, 39(9): 1,359–1,366.

Goleman, D. (1996). *Emotional intelligence*. London: Bloomsbury.

Gottfried, R. S. (1978). *Epidemic disease in fifteenth century England: The medical response and the demographic consequences*. Leicester: Leicester University Press.

Graham, H. (1987). 'Women's smoking and family health'. *Social Science and Medicine*, 25(1): 47–56.

Green, A. (1995). *La Causalité psychique: entre nature et culture*. Paris: Editions Odile Jacob.

Greenwood, G. D. (1994). *Realism, identity and emotion*. London: Sage.

Gregory, J. and Miller, S. (1998). *Science in public: Communication, culture and credibility*. New York: Plenum.

Gussow, Z. (1989). *Leprosy, racism and public health*. San Francisco, CA: Westview.

Haddock, G. and Zanna, M. P. (1998). 'On the use of open-ended measures to assess attitudinal components'. *British Journal of Social Psychology*, 37(2): 129–149.

Haddock, G., Zanna, M. P. and Esses, V. M. (1993). 'Assessing the structure of prejudicial attitudes: The case of attitudes towards homosexuals'. *Journal of Personality and Social Psychology*, 65: 1,105–1,118.

Halbwachs, M. (1950). *The collective memory*, translated from French original (1980). New York: Harper and Row.

Hall, S. and Du Gay, P. (eds.)(1996). *Questions of cultural identity*. London: Sage.

Hall, S. (1980). 'Encoding/decoding', in S. Hall (ed.) *Culture, media, language*. London: Hutchinson.

   (1991). 'Psychoanalysis, identity and difference'. Paper presented at Psychoanalysis and the Public Sphere Conference, University of East London, 1–2 November.

Hansen, W. B., Hahn, G. L. and Wolkenstein, B. H. (1990). 'Perceived personal immunity: Beliefs about susceptibility to AIDS'. *Journal of Sex Research*, 27(4): 622–628.

Harré, R. and Parrott, w. G. (eds.) (1996) *The emotions: social, cultural and biological dimensions*. London: Sage.

Harris, P. (1996). 'Sufficient grounds for optimism? The relationship between perceived controllability and optimistic bias'. *Journal of Social and Clinical Psychology*, 15: 9–52.

Harris, P. and Middleton, W. (1994). 'The illusion of control and optimism about health: On being less at risk but no more in control than others'. *British Journal of Social Psychology*, 33(4): 369–386.

Heider, F. (1958). *The psychology of interpersonal relations*. New York: John Wiley.

Heine, S. J. and Lehman, D. R. (1995). 'The cultural construction of self-enhancement: An examination of group-serving biases'. *Journal of Personality and Social Psychology*, 72(6): 1268–1283.

Henriques, J., Hollway, W., Urwin, C., Venn, C. and Walkerdine, V. (eds.)(1984/1998). *Changing the subject: Psychology, social regulation and subjectivity*. London: Routledge.

Herek, G. M. & Capitano, J. P. (1993). 'Public reactions to AIDS in the United States: A second decade of stigma'. *American Journal of Public Health*, 83(4): 574–577.

Herzlich, C. (1973). *Health and illness*. London: Academic Press.

Herzlich, C., & Pierret, J. (1987). *Illness and self in society*, translated from French original (1984). Baltimore, MD: Johns Hopkins University Press.

   (1989). 'The construction of a social phenomenon: AIDS in the French press'. *Social Science and Medicine*, 29(11): 1,235–1,242.

Hinshelwood, R. D. (1987). *What happens in groups: Psychoanalysis, the individual and the community.* London: Free Association.

(1989a). *A dictionary of Kleinian thought.* London: Free Association.

(1989b). 'Social possession of identity', in B. Richards (ed.) *Crises of the self: Further essays on psychoanalysis and politics.* London: Free Association, pp. 75–83.

Hochschild, A. R. (1998). 'The sociology of emotion as a way of seeing', in G. Bendelow and S. J. Williams (eds.) *Emotions and social life: Critical themes and contemporary issues.* London: Routledge, pp. 3–15.

Holloway, H. C. and Fullerton, C. S. (1994). 'The psychology of terror and its aftermath', in R. J. Ursano, B. G. McCaughey and C. S. Fullerton (eds.) *Individual and community responses to trauma and disaster.* Cambridge: Cambridge University Press, pp. 31–45.

Hollway, W. and Jefferson, T. (1997). 'Eliciting narrative through the in-depth interview'. *Qualitative Enquiry,* 3(1): 53–70.

Hoorens, V. (1994) 'Unrealistic optimism in health and safety risks', in D. R. Rutter and L. Quine (eds.) *Social psychology and health: European perspectives.* Aldershot: Avebury, pp. 153–174.

Holtze, H. (1856). 'Analytical introduction to Count Gobineau's moral and intellectual diversity of the races', in J. A. de gobineau, *The moral and intellectual diversity of races, with particular reference to their respective influence in the civil and political history of mankind.* Philadelphia, PA: Lippincott.

Ichheiser, G. (1943). 'Misinterpretations in everyday life and the psychologist's frame of reference'. *Character and Personality,* 12: 145–160.

Isaacs, G. & McKendrick, B. (1992). *Male homosexuality in South Africa.* Cape Town: Oxford University Press.

Izard, C. E. (1991). *The psychology of emotions.* New York: Plenum.

Jaques, E. (1977). 'Social systems as defence against persecutory and depressive anxiety: A contribution to a psycho-analytical study of social processes', in M. Klein, P. Herman and R. E. Money-Kyrle (eds.) *New directions in psychoanalysis.* London: Maresfield Reprints, pp. 478–498.

Jaspers, J. M. and Fraser, C. (1984). 'Attitudes and social representations', in R. M. Farr and S. Moscovici (eds.) *Social representations.* Cambridge: Cambridge University Press, pp. 101–123.

Jodelet, D. (1991). *Madness and social representations.* London: Harvester Wheatsheaf.

Joffe, H. (1995). 'Social representations of AIDS: Towards encompassing issues of power'. *Papers on Social Representations,* 4(1): 29–40.

(1996a). 'AIDS research and prevention: A social representational approach'. *British Journal of Medical Psychology,* 69 (3): 169–190.

(1996b) 'The shock of the new: A psycho-dynamic extension of social representations theory'. *Journal for the Theory of Social Behaviour,* 26(2): 197–219.

(1997a). 'Intimacy and love in late modern conditions: Implications for unsafe sexual practices', in J. M. Ussher (ed.) *Body talk.* London: Routledge, pp. 159–175.

(1997b). 'Juxtaposing positivist and non-positivist approaches to social scientific AIDS research'. *British Journal of Medical Psychology,* 70(1): 75–83.

Jovchelovitch, S. & Gervais, M-C. (1999). 'Social representations of health and illness: The case of the Chinese community in England'. *Journal of Community and Applied Social Psychology.*

Kaes, R. (1980). *L'Ideologie – etudes psychanalytiques: mentalité de l'idéal et esprit de corps.* Paris: Dunod.

———— (1984). 'Representation and mentalisation: From the represented group to the group process', in R. M. Farr and S. Moscovici (eds.) *Social representations.* Cambridge: Cambridge University Press, pp. 361–377.

Karpas, A. (1990). 'Origin and spread of AIDS'. *Nature,* 348: 578.

Kelley, H. H. (1973). 'The process of causal attribution', *American Psychologist,* 28: 107–128.

Kihlstrom, J. F. (1987). The cognitive unconscious. *Science,* 237: 1,445–1,452.

Kitzinger, J. & Miller, D. (1991). *In black and white.* Medical Research Council Working Paper no. 27, in association with the Glasgow University Media Group.

Klein, M. (1929). 'Infantile anxiety situations reflected in a work of art and in the creative impulse'. *International Journal of Psycho-Analysis,* 10: 436–443.

———— (1946). 'Notes on some schizoid mechanisms'. *International Journal of Psycho-Analysis,* 27: 99–110.

———— (1952). 'Some theoretical conclusions regarding the emotional life of the infant', in M. Klein, P. Hemann, S. Isaacs and J. Riviere (eds.) *Developments in psycho-analysis.* London: Hogarth, pp. 198–236.

Kleinhesselink, R. R. and Rosa, E. A. (1991). 'Cognitive representations of risk perceptions: A comparison of Japan and the United States'. *Journal of Cross Cultural Psychology,* 22: 11–28.

Kristeva, J. (1991). *Strangers to ourselves,* trans. L. S. Roudiez. London: Harvester Wheatsheaf.

Lacey, C. J. N. & Waugh, M. A. (1983). 'Cellular immunity in male homosexuals'. *Lancet,* 2: 464.

Landman, J. (1996). 'Social control of "negative" emotions: the case of regret', in R. Harré and W. G. Parrott (eds.) *The emotions: Social, cultural and biological dimensions.* London: Sage, pp. 89–116.

Langer, E. J. (1975) 'The illusion of control'. *Journal of Personality and Social Psychology,* 32: 311–328.

Latour, B. & Woolgar, S. (1979). *Laboratory life: The social construction of scientific facts.* Beverly Hills, CA: Sage.

Lazarus, R. S. (1991). 'Cognition and motivation in emotion'. *American Psychologist,* 46(4): 352–367.

Le Bon, G. (1895). *Les Lois psychologiques de l'evolution des peuples.* Paris: Alcan.

LeDoux, J. (1998). *The emotional brain.* London: Weidenfeld and Nicolson.

Lee, T. R., MacDonald, S. M. and Coote, J. A. (1993). 'Perceptions of risk and attitudes to safety at a nuclear reprocessing plant'. Paper presented at Society for Risk Assessment, Fourth Conference, October, Rome.

Lek, Y-Y. and Bishop, G. D. (1995). 'Perceived vulnerability to illness threats:Tthe role of disease type, risk factor perception and attributions.' *Psychology and Health,* 10(3): 205–217.

Lerner, M. J. (1980). *The belief in a just world.* New York: Plenum.

Leventhal, H. (1980). 'Toward a comprehensive theory of emotion', in L.

Berkowitz (ed.) *Advances in experimental social psychology* (vol. 13). New York: Academic Press.

Leventhal, H. & Nerenz, D. R. (1985). 'The assessment of illness cognition', in P. Karoly (ed.) *Measurement strategies in health psychology.* New York: John Wiley, pp. 517–554.

Leventhal, H., Benyamini, Y., Brownlee, S., Diefenbach, M., Leventhal, E. A., Patrick-Miller, L. & Robitaille, C. (1997). 'Illness representations: Theoretical foundations', in K. J. Petrie & J. A. Weinman (eds.) *Perceptions of health and illness: Current research and applications.* Singapore: Harwood Academic, pp. 19–45.

Lévi-Strauss, C. (1967). *The savage mind.* Chicago: University of Chicago Press.

Long, E. (1774). *The history of Jamaica.* London: Lowndes.

Lupton, D. (1997). 'Psychoanalytic sociology and the medical encounter: Parsons and beyond'. *Sociology of Health and Illness,* 19(5): 561–578.

Lutz, C. A. (1996). 'Engendered emotion: Gender, power and rhetoric of emotional control in American discourse', in R. Harré and W. G. Parrott (eds.) *The emotions: Social, cultural and biological dimensions.* London: Sage, pp. 151–170.

McCann Group (1988). *AIDS: Awareness, attitudes pre and post the advertising campaign* (control number: 002/88, June). Johannesburg, South Africa: McCann Group.

McCulloch, J. (1995). *Colonial psychiatry and 'the African mind'.* Cambridge: Cambridge University Press.

Maiman, L. A. and Becker, M. H. (1974). *The Health Belief Model: Origin and correlates in psychological theory.* New Jersey: Charles Slack.

Malloy, T. E., Fisher, W. A., Albright, L., Misovich, S. J. and Fisher, J. D. (1997). 'Interpersonal perception of the AIDS risk potential of persons of the opposite sex'. *Health Psychology,* 16(5): 480–486.

Manstead, A. S. R. and Parker, D. (1996). 'Reconstructing the theory of planned behaviour'. Paper presented at the Eleventh General Meeting of the European Association of Experimental Social Psychology, Gmunden, Austria, 13–18 July.

Manstead, A. S. R., Parker, D., Stradling, S. G. and Lawton, R. (1995). 'Adding affect to the theory of planned behaviour'. Paper based on the research report for the United Kingdom Department of Transport, London.

Markova, I. and Wilkie, P. (1987). 'Representations, concepts and social change: The phenomenon of AIDS'. *Journal for the Theory of Social Behaviour,* 17(4): 389–409.

Markova, I., McKee, K. J., Power, K. G. and Moodie, E. (1995). 'The self and the Other: Perceptions of the risk of HIV/AIDS in Scottish Prisons', in R. M. Farr and I. Markova (eds.) *Representations of health, illness and handicap.* Chur, Switzerland: Harwood Academic, pp. 111–129.

Marks, D. F. (1996). 'Health psychology in context'. *Journal of Health Psychology,* 1: 7–21.

Mearns, K. and Flin, R. (1996). 'Risk perception in hazardous industries'. *The Psychologist,* 9(9): 401–404.

Meissner, W. W. (1989). 'Projection and projective identification', in J. Sandler (ed.) *Projection, identification, projective identification.* London: Karnac, pp. 27–49.

Menzies-Lyth, I. (1960). 'The functioning of a social system as a defence against anxiety'. *Human Relations,* 11: 95–121.

(1989). *The dynamics of the social.* London: Free Association.

Merleau-Ponty, M. (1962). *The phenomenology of perception.* London: Routledge.

Mestrovic, S. G. (1997). *Postemotional society.* London: Sage.

Michael, M. (1994). 'Discourse and uncertainty: Postmodern variations'. *Theory and Psychology,* 4(3): 383–404.

Minogue, K. (1998). *The silencing of society: The true cost of the lust for news.* London: Social Affairs Unit.

Mol, A. P. J. and Spaargaren, G. (1993). 'Environment, modernity and the risk-society: The apocalyptic horizon of environmental reform'. *International Sociology,* 8(4): 431–459.

Montgomery, S. B., Joseph, J. G., Becker, M. H., Ostrow, D. G., Kessler, R. C. and Kirscht, J. P. (1989). 'The Health Belief Model in understanding compliance with preventive recommendations for AIDS: How useful?' *AIDS Education and Prevention,* 1 (4): 303–323.

Morris, R. J. (1976). *Cholera 1832: A social response to an epidemic.* London: Croom Helm.

Morton, R. S. (1971). *Sexual freedom and venereal disease.* London: Owen.

Moscovici, S. (1961/1976). *La Psychanalyse, son image et son public.* Paris: Presses Universitaires de France.

(1982). 'The coming era of representations', in J. P. Codol & J. P. Leyens (eds.). *Cognitive approaches to social behaviour.* La Haye: Nijhoff, pp. 115–150.

(1984a). 'The myth of the lonely paradigm: A rejoinder'. *Social Research,* 51: 939–969.

(1984b). 'The phenomenon of social representations', in R. M. Farr and S. Moscovici (eds.) *Social representations.* Cambridge: Cambridge University Press, pp. 3–70.

(1985). *The age of the crowd: A historical treatise on mass psychology.* Cambridge: Cambridge University Press.

(1987). 'Answers and questions'. *Journal for the Theory of Social Behaviour,* 17(4): 513–528.

Moses, R. (1989). 'Projection, identification and projective identification: Their relation to political process', in J. Sandler (ed.) *Projection, identification, projective identification.* London: Karnac, pp. 133–150.

Myers, L. and Brewin, C. (1996). 'Illusions of well-being and the repressive coping style'. *British Journal of Social Psychology,* 35: 443–457.

Nelkin, D. & Gilman, S. L. (1988). 'Placing blame for devastating disease'. *Social Research,* 55(3): 361–378.

Ngubane, H. (1977). *Body and mind in Zulu medicine.* London: Academic Press.

Norris, F. H. (1997). 'Frequency and structure of precautionary behaviour in the domains of hazard preparedness, crime prevention, vehicular safety, and health maintenance'. *Health Psychology,* 16(6): 566–575.

Oatley, K. (1998). 'Emotion'. *The Psychologist,* 11(6): 285–288.

Offir, J. T., Fisher, J. D., Williams, S. S. and Fisher, W. A. (1993). 'Reasons for inconsistent AIDS-preventive behaviours among gay men'. *Journal of Sex Research*, 30(1): 62–69.

Oliver-Smith, A. (1996). 'Anthropological research on hazards and disasters'. *Annual Review of Anthropology*, 25: 303–328.

Otten, W. and van der Pligt, J. (1996) 'Contextual effects in the measurement of comparative optimism in probability judgements'. *Journal Social and Clinical Psychology*, 15(1): 80–101.

Paez, D. and Echebarria, A. (1989). 'Social representations and memory: The case of AIDS'. *European Journal of Social Psychology*, 19: 543–551.

Paez, D., Echebarria, A., Valencia, J., Romo, I., San Juan, C. and Vergara, A. (1991). 'AIDS social representations: Contents and processes'. *Journal of Community and Applied Social Psychology*, 1: 89–104.

Parrott, W. G. and Harré, R. (1996) 'Overview', in R. Harré and W. G. Parrott (eds.) *The emotions: Social, cultural and biological dimensions.* London: Sage, pp. 1–20.

Peeters, G., Cammaert, M-F. and Czapinski, J. (1997). 'Unrealistic optimism and positive-negative asymmetry: A conceptual and cross-cultural study of interrelationships between optimism, pessimism and realism'. *International Journal of Psychology*, 32(1): 23–34.

Perloff, L. S. and Fetzer, B. K. (1986). 'Self–other judgements and perceived vulnerability of victimization'. *Journal of Personality and Social Psychology*, 50: 502–510.

Phillips, A. (1988). *Winnicott.* Cambridge, MA: Harvard University Press.
    (1995). *Terror and experts.* London: Faber and Faber.

Pitts, M. (1996). *The psychology of preventive health.* London: Routledge.

Porto, M. P. D. and Defreitas, C. M. (1996). 'Major chemical accidents in industrialising countries: The socio-political amplification of risk'. *Risk Analysis*, 16(1): 19–29.

Potter, J. and Litton, I. (1985) 'Some problems underlying the theory of social representations'. *British Journal of Social Psychology*, 24: 81–90.

Radley, A. (1999). 'Blame, abhorrence and the social response to suffering'. *Health*, 3: 167–187.

Regan, P. C., Snyder, M. and Kassin, S. M. (1995). 'Unrealistic optimism: self-enhancement or person positivity'. *Personality and Social Psychology Bulletin*, 21(10): 1,073–1,082.

Rogers, N. (1992). *Dirt and disease: Polio before FDR.* New Brunswick, NJ: Rutgers University Press.

Rose, D., Efraim, D., Gervais, M-C., Joffe, H., Jovchelovitch, S. and Morant, N. (1995). 'Questioning consensus in social representations theory'. *Papers on Social Representations*, 4(2): 150–155.

Rosebury, T. (1972). *Microbes and morals.* London: Secker and Warburg.

Ross, L. (1977). 'The intuitive psychologist and his shortcomings: Distortions in the attribution process', in L. Berkowitz (ed.) *Advances in experimental social psychology*, vol. 10. New York: Academic Press, pp. 174–220.

Russell, G. W. and Mentzel, R. K. (1990). 'Sympathy and altruism in response to disasters'. *Journal of Social Psychology*, 130(3): 309–316.

Rustin, M. (1995). 'Lacan, Klein and politics: The positive and negative in psychoanalytic thought', in A. Elliott and S. Frosh (eds.) *Psychoanalysis in contexts*. London: Routledge, pp. 223–245.

Sabatier, R. (1988). *Blaming others: Prejudice, race and worldwide AIDS*. London: Panos Institute.

Said, E. W. (1978). *Orientalism: Western conceptions of the Orient*. London: Routledge.

Sandler, J. (ed.) (1989) *Projection, identification, projective identification*. London: Karnac.

Schachter, S. and Singer, J. E. (1962). 'Cognitive, social and physiological determinants of emotional state'. *Psychological Review*, 69: 379–399.

Segal, H. (1995). 'From Hiroshima to the Gulf War and after: A psychoanalytic perspective', in A. Elliott and S. Frosh (eds.) *Psychoanalysis in contexts*. London: Routledge, pp. 191–204.

Segerstrom, S. C., Taylor, S. S., Kemeny, M. E. and Fahey, J. L. (1998). 'Optimism is associated with mood, coping, and immune change in response to stress'. *Journal of Personality and Social Psychology*, 74(6): 1646–1655.

Shaver, K. G. and Drown, D. (1986). 'On causality, responsibility and self-blame: A theoretical note'. *Journal of Personality and Social Psychology*, 50(4): 699–702.

Sherwood, R. (1980). *The psychodynamics of race*. Brighton: Harvester.

Silverman, D. (1993). *Interpreting qualitative data: Methods for analysing text, talk and interaction*. London: Sage.

Simmel, G. (1903/1971). 'The Metropolis and mental life', in D. N. Levine (ed.) *On individuality and social forms: Selected writings*. Chicago: University of Chicago Press, pp. 324–339.

Sjoberg, P. and Drottz-Sjoberg, M-B. (1991). 'Knowledge and risk perception among nuclear power plant employees'. *Risk Analysis*, 11: 607–618.

Sloan, T. (1996). *Damaged life: The crisis of the modern psyche*. London: Routledge.

Smith, J. A., Flowers, P. and Osborne, M. (1997). 'Interpretative phenomenological anaylsis and the psychology of health and illness', in L. Yardley (ed.) *Material discourses of health and illness*. London: Routledge, pp. 68–91.

Sobo, E. J. (1995). *Choosing unsafe sex: AIDS-risk denial among disadvantaged women*. Philadelphia: University of Pennsylvania Press.

Sontag, S. (1979). *Illness as metaphor*. New York: Vintage Books.

——— (1989). *AIDS and its metaphors*. London: Allen Lane.

Stainton-Rogers, W. (1996). 'Critical approaches to health psychology'. *Journal of Health Psychology*, 1: 65–77.

Stallybrass, P. and White, A. (1986). *The politics and poetics of transgression*. Ithaca, NY: Cornell University Press.

Stearns, P. N. and Knapp, M. (1996). 'Historical perspectives on grief', in R. Harré and W. G. Parrott (eds.) *The emotions: Social, cultural and biological dimensions*. London: Sage, pp. 132–150.

Stimson, G. V., Donoghue, M., Alldritt, L. and Dolan, K. (1988). 'HIV risk transmission behaviour of clients attending syringe exchange schemes in England and Scotland'. *British Journal of Addiction*, 83: 1,449–1,455.

Strongman, K. T. (1996). *The psychology of emotion: Theories of emotion in perspective*. Chichester: John Wiley.

Sutherland, S. (1997). 'Tales of memory and imagination'. *Nature*, 388: 239.

Tajfel, H. & Turner, J. C. (1979). 'An integrative theory of intergroup conflict', in W. G. Austin & S. Worchel (eds.) *The social psychology of intergroup relations*. Monterey, CA: Brooks/Cole, pp. 33–47.

Taylor, S. E. (1989). *Positive illusions*. New York: Basic Books.

Taylor, S. E. and Armor, D. A. (1996). 'Positive illusions and coping with adversity'. *Journal of Personality*, 64(4): 873–898.

Taylor, S. E. and Brown, J. D. (1988) 'Illusion and well-being: A social psychological perspective on mental health'. *Psychological Bulletin*, 103: 193–210.

(1994) ' "Illusion" of mental health does not explain positive illusions'. *American Psychologist*, 49(11): 972–973.

Taylor, S. E., Kemeny, M. E., Aspinwall, L. G., Schneider, S. C., Rodriguez, R. and Herbert, M. (1992). 'Optimism, coping, psychological distress, and high-risk sexual behaviour among men at risk of AIDS'. *Journal of Personality and Social Psychology*, 63: 460–473.

Temperley, J. (1989). 'Psychoanalysis and the threat of nuclear war', in B. Richards (ed.) *Crises of the self: Further essays on psychoanalysis and politics*. London: Free Association, pp. 259–267.

Tennen, H. and Affleck, G. (1990). 'Blaming others for threatening events'. *Psychological Bulletin*, 108(2): 209–232.

Tester, K. (1998). ' "Bored and blase": Television, the emotions and Georg Simmel', in G. Bendelow and S. J. Williams (eds.) *Emotions and social life: Critical themes and contemporary issues*. London: Routledge, pp. 83–96.

Treichler, P. A. (1989). 'AIDS and HIV infection in the third world: A first world chronicle', in B. Kruger & P. Mariani (eds.) *Remaking history*. Seattle, WA: Bay Press.

Trevisan, J. S. (1986). *Perverts in paradise*, trans. M. Foreman. London: GMP.

Ursano, R. J., McCaughey, B. G. and Fullerton, C. S. (eds.) (1994) *Individual and community responses to trauma and disaster*. Cambridge: Cambridge University Press.

Ussher, J. (ed.) (1996) 'Premenstrual syndrome: Reconciling disciplinary divides through the adoption of a material-discursive epistemological standpoint'. *Annual Review of Sex Research*, 7: 218–251.

(1997) *Body talk*. London: Routledge.

Vass, A. A. (1986). *AIDS: A plague in us*. St Ives, Cambs.: Venus Academica.

Verkuyten, M. (1995). 'Symbols and social representations'. *Journal for the Theory of Social Behaviour*, 25(3): 263–284.

Wagner, W., Lahnsteiner, I. & Elejabarrieta, F. (1995). 'How the sperm dominates the ovum: Objectification by metaphor in the social representation of conception'. *European Journal of Social Psychology*, 25: 671–688.

Walster, E. (1966). 'Assignment of responsibility for an accident'. *Journal of Personality and Social Psychology*, 3(1): 73–79.

Watney, S. (1987). *Policing desire*. London: Comedia.

(1989). 'Missionary positions: AIDS, "Africa" and Race'. *Differences*, 1(1): 83–100.

Watts, M. W. (1996). 'Political xenophobia and the transition from socialism:

Threat, racism and ideology among East German youth'. *Political Psychology*, 17(1): 97–126.

Weinberg, M. and Williams, C. (1988). 'Black sexuality: A test of two theories'. *Journal of Sex Research*, 25(2): 197–218.

Weiner, B. (1980). 'A cognitive (attribution)-emotion-action model of motivated behaviour: An analysis of judgements of help-giving'. *Journal of Personality and Social Psychology*, 39(2): 186–200.

Weinstein, N. D. (1980). 'Unrealistic optimism about future life events'. *Journal of Personality and Social Psychology*, 39: 806–820.

(1982). 'Unrealistic optimism about susceptibility to health problems'. *Journal of Behavioural Medicine*, 5: 441–460.

(1987). 'Unrealistic optimism about susceptibility to health problems: Conclusions from a community wide sample'. *Journal of Behavioral Medicine*, 10: 481–495.

Weinstein, N. D. and Klein, W. M. (1996). 'Unrealistic optimism: Present and future'. Special issue *Journal of Social and Clinical Psychology*, 15(1): 1–8.

Weiss, R. A. and Wrangham, R. W. (1999). From *Pan* to pandemic. *Nature*, 397: 385–386.

Wellings, K. (1988). 'Perceptions of risk', in P. Aggleton & H. Homans (eds.) *Social aspects of AIDS*. London: Falmer, pp. 83–105.

Wetherall, M. and Potter, J. (1992). *Mapping the language of racism*. London: Harvester Wheatsheaf.

Wierzbicka, A. (1994). 'Emotion, language and cultural scripts', in S. Kitayama and H. R. Markus (eds.) *Emotions and culture: Empirical studies in mutual influence*. Washington, DC: American Psychological Society, pp. 133–196.

Wilkinson, R. G. (1996). *Unhealthy societies: The afflictions of inequality*. London: Routledge.

Williams, G. (1993). 'Chronic illness and the pursuit of virtue in everyday life', in A. Radley (ed.) *Worlds of illness: Biographical and cultural perspectives on health and disease*. London: Routledge, pp. 92–108.

Williams, S. J. (1998). 'Emotions, cyberspace and the "virtual" body: A critical appraisal', in G. Bendelow and S. J. Williams (eds.) *Emotions and social life: Critical themes and contemporary issues*. London: Routledge, pp. 120–132.

Williams, S. J. and Bendelow, G. (1998). 'Introduction: Emotions in social life', in G. Bendelow and S. J. Williams (eds.) *Emotions and social life: Critical themes and contemporary issues*. London: Routledge, pp. xv–xxx.

Winnicott, D. W. (1958). *Collected papers: Through paediatrics to psychoanalysis*. New York: Basic Books.

Withey, S. B. (1962). 'Reaction to uncertain threat', in G. W. Baker and D. W. Chapman (eds.) *Man and society in disaster*. New York: Basic Books, pp. 93–123.

Wynne, B. (1982). *Rationality and ritual: The Windscale Inquiry and nuclear decisions in Britain*. Chalfont St Giles: British Society for the History of Science.

(1995). 'Public understanding of science', in S. Jasanoff, G. E. Markle, J. C. Petersen and T. Pinch (eds.) *Handbook of science and technology studies*. London: Sage, pp. 361–388.

(1996). 'May the sheep safely graze? A reflexive view of the expert–lay knowledge divide', in S. Lash, B. Szerszynski and B. Wynne (eds.) *Risk, environment and modernity: Towards a new ecology*. London: Sage, pp. 44–83.

Yardley, L. (ed.) (1997). *Material discourses of health and illness*. London: Routledge.

Young, R. J. C. (1995). *Colonial desire: Hybridity in theory, culture and race*. London: Routledge.

Young, R. M. (1996). 'Is "perversion" obsolete?' *Psychology in Society*, 21: 5–26.

Zajonc, R. (1980). 'Feeling and thinking: Preferences need no inferences'. *American Psychologist*, 35: 151–175.

Zimolong, B. (1985). 'Hazard perception and risk estimation in accident causation', in R. E. Eberts and C. G. Eberts (eds.) *Trends in ergonomics/human factors II*. Amsterdam: Elsevier Science, pp. 463–470.

Index

responsibility (*cont.*)
  see also blame; conspiracy theories; 'not me–other' response to risk; scapegoating
risk
  changing representations of, 126–32, 134–5, 143–4
  control of, 3–5
  experienced via media, 120–1, 122
  internalised by marginalised groups, 46
  responses to: affective dimension of, 6–7, 109–10; approaches to, 7–13, 14–16; cognitive approach, 7–8; features of good theory, 139–41; overarching theory, 141–3; psycho–dynamic theory, 11, 79–88, 99–105, 127; social representations theory, 9–11, 99–105; subjectivity in, 8–9; *see also* AIDS/HIV; 'not me–other' response to risk; optimistic bias
  scientific assessments of, 60–1
risk society, nature of, 2–7
risks, compared with hazards, 142

Said, E.W., 18–19, 27–8
scapegoating, 26–7, 32–3
science
  lay people's understanding of, 9–10, 51
  natural science model, 139–40
  representations of crises, 33
  values in, 93
scientific knowledge, transformation of, 92–6
scientists
  assessment of risk by, 60–1
  as focus of AIDS conspiracy theories, 47–9
  responses to AIDS, 42–4
  see also experts
self–report data, 110–12, 115
sexual practices, and representations of AIDS, 40–1, 43
sexuality
  and blame for epidemics, 25
  and concept of 'other', 20–1, 35
  link with disaster, 23–4
  and social representations, 91
  and women as cause of illness, 28
  women's optimistic bias and, 62–3
  see also gay men; homosexuality
Shaver, K.G., 67
sin
  link with disaster, 24
  and representations of AIDS, 40–1, 43, 49, 76
Sobo, E.J., 62–3

social constructionist approach to emotion, 113–14
Social Identity Theory (SIT), 80
social psychology, good theory in, 139–41
social representations
  changing, 105–6, 126–32, 134–5, 143–4
  environmental influences on, 133
  motivation for formation of, 34, 96–8
  nature of, 91
  processes in formation of, 92–6
  role in risk response, 133–4
  social nature of, 98–9
social representations theory
  critiques of, 137–9
  nature of, 9–11, 90–1, 127–8
social representations–psycho–dynamic approach, 99–105
social science
  application of psychodynamic theory to, 83–8
  assumptions of, 140–1
sociocultural approaches to emotion, 116–22
sociohistorical processes, and psycho–dynamic theory, 79–83
sociology, study of emotion, 117–18
'spinning', 119
spirit possession, 28
splitting
  nature of, 11, 73–9, 88, 99, 132–3
  role of social forces in, 79–81
  stage following, 128–9, 134
Stimson, G.V., 63
subjectivity
  study of, 86, 110
  in study of emotion, 108–9, 110
  in study of risk, 8–9
symbolisation, 95–6
  responses to risk, 6–7
syphilis, 25, 33
  Tuskegee Study, 49, 50

Taylor, S.E., 61–2
Tester, K., 120
theory, features of good theory, 139–41
Theory of Planned Behaviour (TPB), 109
threat, experienced via media, 120–1
Tuskegee Study, 49, 50

Ursano, R.J., 31

war
  and AIDS conspiracy theories, 49
  perceived risk of, 31–2
  symbolisation of, 96
Weinstein, N.D., 60, 61